Interesting School Facts	2
Do You Spend Wisely?	4
It Feels So Good to Give!	6
Where Did Time Learn to Fly?	8
There Are So Many Fun Things to Do!	10
Don't You Just Love Dogs?	12
Cool Off at Camp in the Summertime!	14
Money Really Adds Up Fast!	16
Oh Boy, It's Time for a Field Trip!	18
Made and Designed 100% by Kids!	20
Let's Go See "America the Beautiful!"	22
We Have Engine Ignition and Lift-off!	24
There's Learning Outside the Classroom Too!	26
Business Is Booming Today!	28
Clubs Are So Much Fun!	30
Decimals Can Be Simply Delightful!	32
Fractions Do Add Up!	34
It's Incredibly Amazing That Fractions Can Be Subtracted!	36
Homework; It's Part of a Kid's Life!	38
Aren't You Glad That $\frac{3}{4}$ of the Earth Is Covered with Water!	40
Let's Try Some Coordinate Geometric Fractions!	42
There's Math in Foods Too!	44
How Long, How Tall, How Far?	46
Let's Get Into Sports!	48
Aren't Reptiles Just the Cutest Things?	50
Head 'Em Up, It's Time to Hike!	52
How Far Is it Going to Be?	54
Art Is Such a Great Way to Express Yourself!	56
Can You Really Take a "Part" of Something from a "Whole" of Something?	58
If You've Got a Choice, Pick Science!	60
It's Time to Pack Your Tent!	62
Multiplying Mixed Numbers Will Not Mix You Up!	64
Let's Measure It and Then Make It!	66
Food and Division Were Meant for Each Other!	68
Here's a Chance to Prove Yourself!	70
Help-at-Home Activities	72

© 2006 Frank Schaffer Publications   1   0-88012-863-1

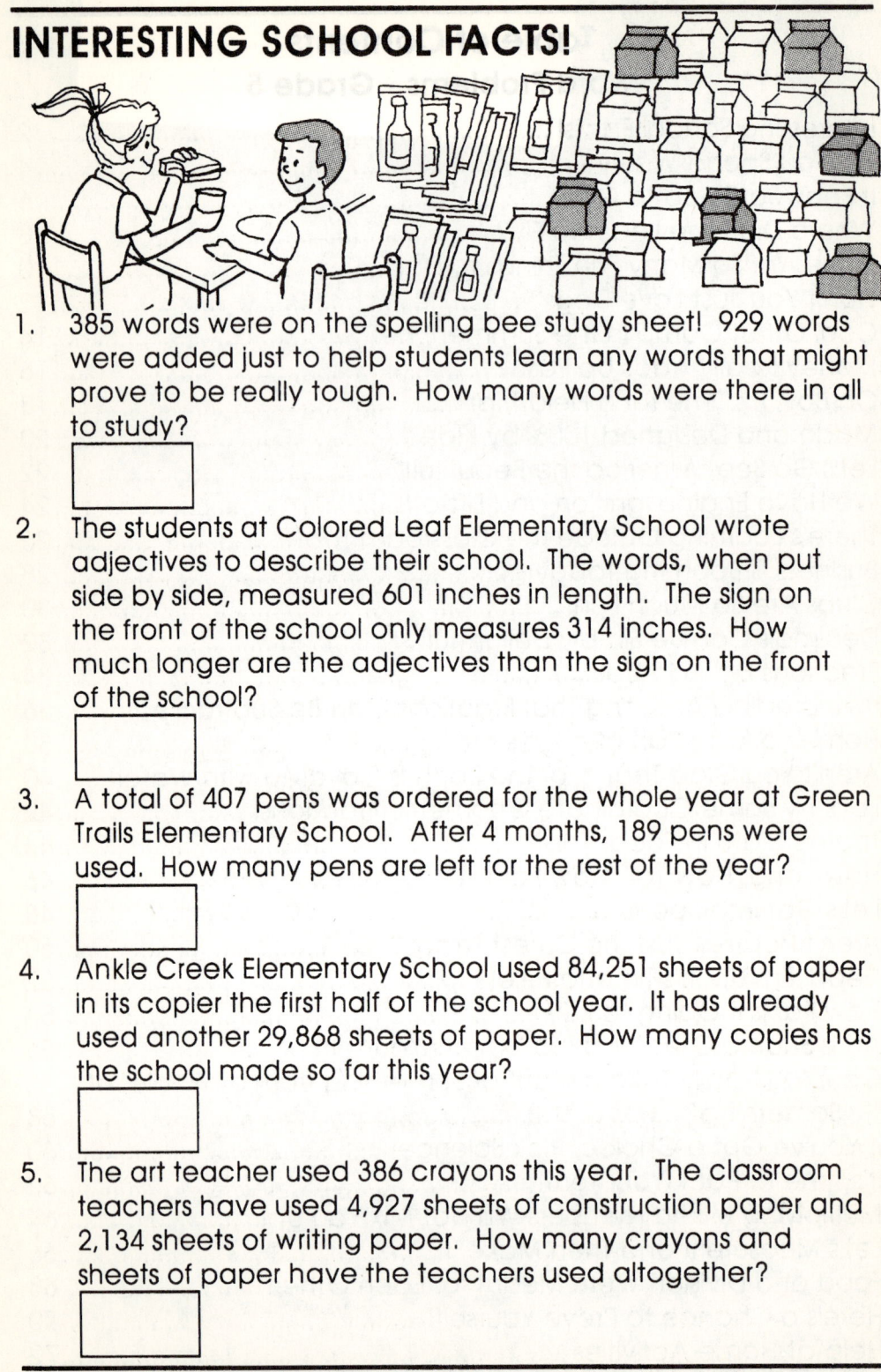

INTERESTING SCHOOL FACTS!

1. 385 words were on the spelling bee study sheet! 929 words were added just to help students learn any words that might prove to be really tough. How many words were there in all to study?

2. The students at Colored Leaf Elementary School wrote adjectives to describe their school. The words, when put side by side, measured 601 inches in length. The sign on the front of the school only measures 314 inches. How much longer are the adjectives than the sign on the front of the school?

3. A total of 407 pens was ordered for the whole year at Green Trails Elementary School. After 4 months, 189 pens were used. How many pens are left for the rest of the year?

4. Ankle Creek Elementary School used 84,251 sheets of paper in its copier the first half of the school year. It has already used another 29,868 sheets of paper. How many copies has the school made so far this year?

5. The art teacher used 386 crayons this year. The classroom teachers have used 4,927 sheets of construction paper and 2,134 sheets of writing paper. How many crayons and sheets of paper have the teachers used altogether?

© 2006 Frank Schaffer Publications 0-88012-863-1

Addition and Subtraction of Whole Numbers

6. During the hot months, the students at Corn Cob Elementary School drink 6,242 gallons of water. During the cold months, they only drink 3,891 gallons. How many more gallons of water do they drink during the hot months?

7. Stuart learned that his school used 83,203 sheets of notebook paper this year. He also found out that his school used 12,419 sheets of drawing paper. How many more sheets of notebook paper were used?

8. The cafeteria ordered 9,234 packets of ketchup, 1,328 pints of orange juice and 3,845 pints of milk. What was the total number of items that the cafeteria ordered?

9. Rose Elementary School is in a city with a population of 592,840. The neighboring city, which always challenges Rose in the statewide band festivals, has a population of 239,284. How many more people live in the city where Rose Elementary School is located?

10. 132,578 students go to school in Jack's town, and 324,954 students go to school in Terry's town. What is the total number of students?

11. To build the new multi-purpose room, 234,846 bricks were delivered. To build the cafeteria, only 97,256 bricks were brought in. How many more bricks were delivered to build the multi-purpose room?

DO YOU SPEND WISELY?

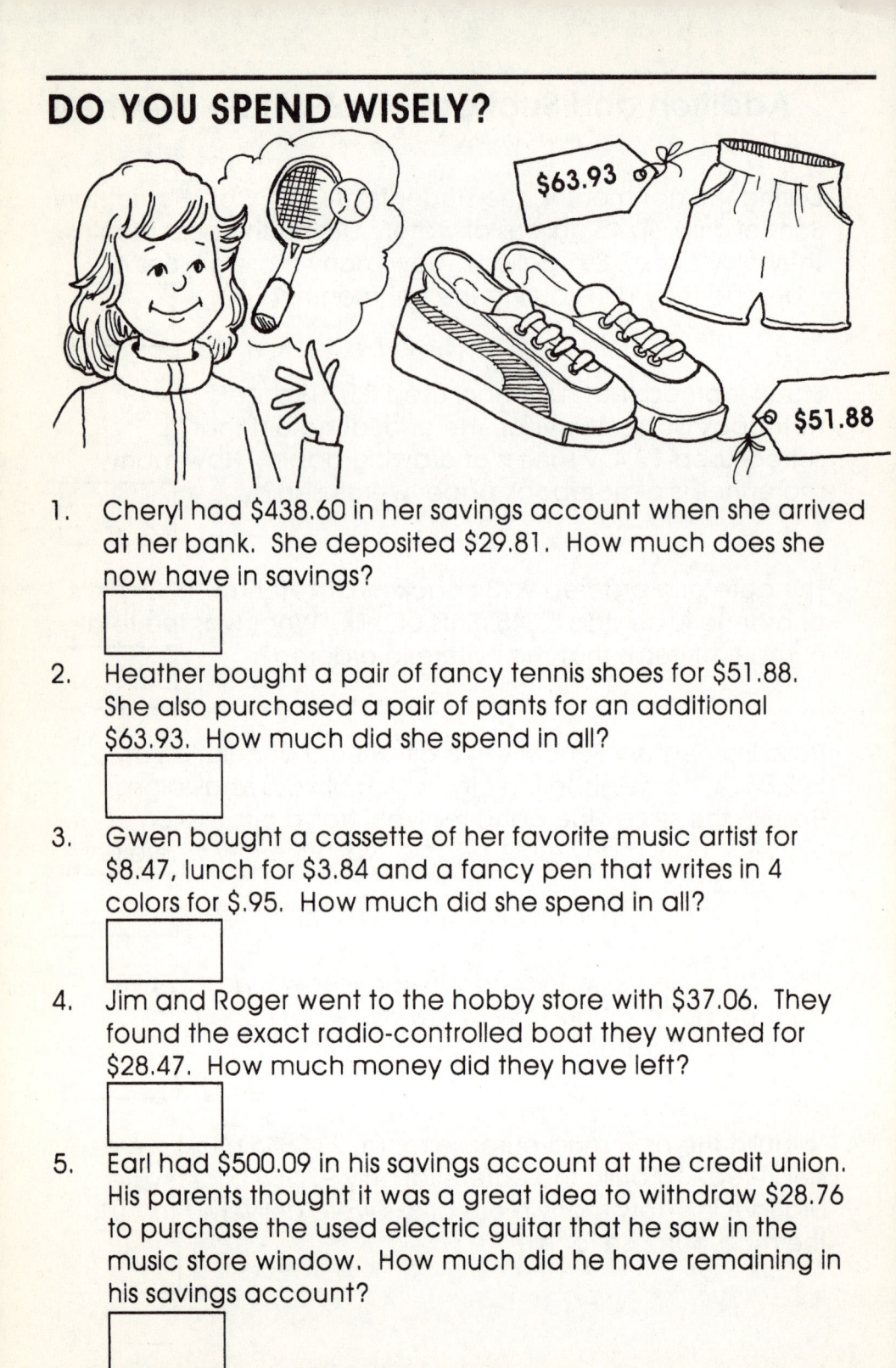

1. Cheryl had $438.60 in her savings account when she arrived at her bank. She deposited $29.81. How much does she now have in savings?

2. Heather bought a pair of fancy tennis shoes for $51.88. She also purchased a pair of pants for an additional $63.93. How much did she spend in all?

3. Gwen bought a cassette of her favorite music artist for $8.47, lunch for $3.84 and a fancy pen that writes in 4 colors for $.95. How much did she spend in all?

4. Jim and Roger went to the hobby store with $37.06. They found the exact radio-controlled boat they wanted for $28.47. How much money did they have left?

5. Earl had $500.09 in his savings account at the credit union. His parents thought it was a great idea to withdraw $28.76 to purchase the used electric guitar that he saw in the music store window. How much did he have remaining in his savings account?

© 2006 Frank Schaffer Publications

Addition and Subtraction of Money

6. Marlene's parents had $8,512.24 saved for their family vacation. The airline tickets cost $743.06. How much did they have left to spend?

7. Jim's parents purchased a synthesizer for him that cost $924.31. They also bought him a music book for $8.95 and a power supply for $36.24. How much did his parents spend altogether so that Jim could begin making music?

8. Jake went to the toy store with $60.42. After much thought and contemplation, he decided to buy the model space shuttle kit for $9.38. How much money did he have left?

9. As Kathleen walked to the mall with her allowance of $6.47, she came across a nickel and 4 pennies lying on the ground. How much money does she have now to spend?

10. Mary had $.89 in her pocket to buy a drink on the way home from school. The drink she chose cost $.43. How much did she have left?

11. Viola bought a comb for $.84, neon shoelaces for $2.47 and, with her parents permission, a new bike for $64.39. How much did she spend in all?

12. The Little family had $589.04 to spend on a new TV. The one that the family fell in love with only sold for $96.83. How much was left to spend on other things like VCR's and portable CD players?

IT FEELS SO GOOD TO GIVE!

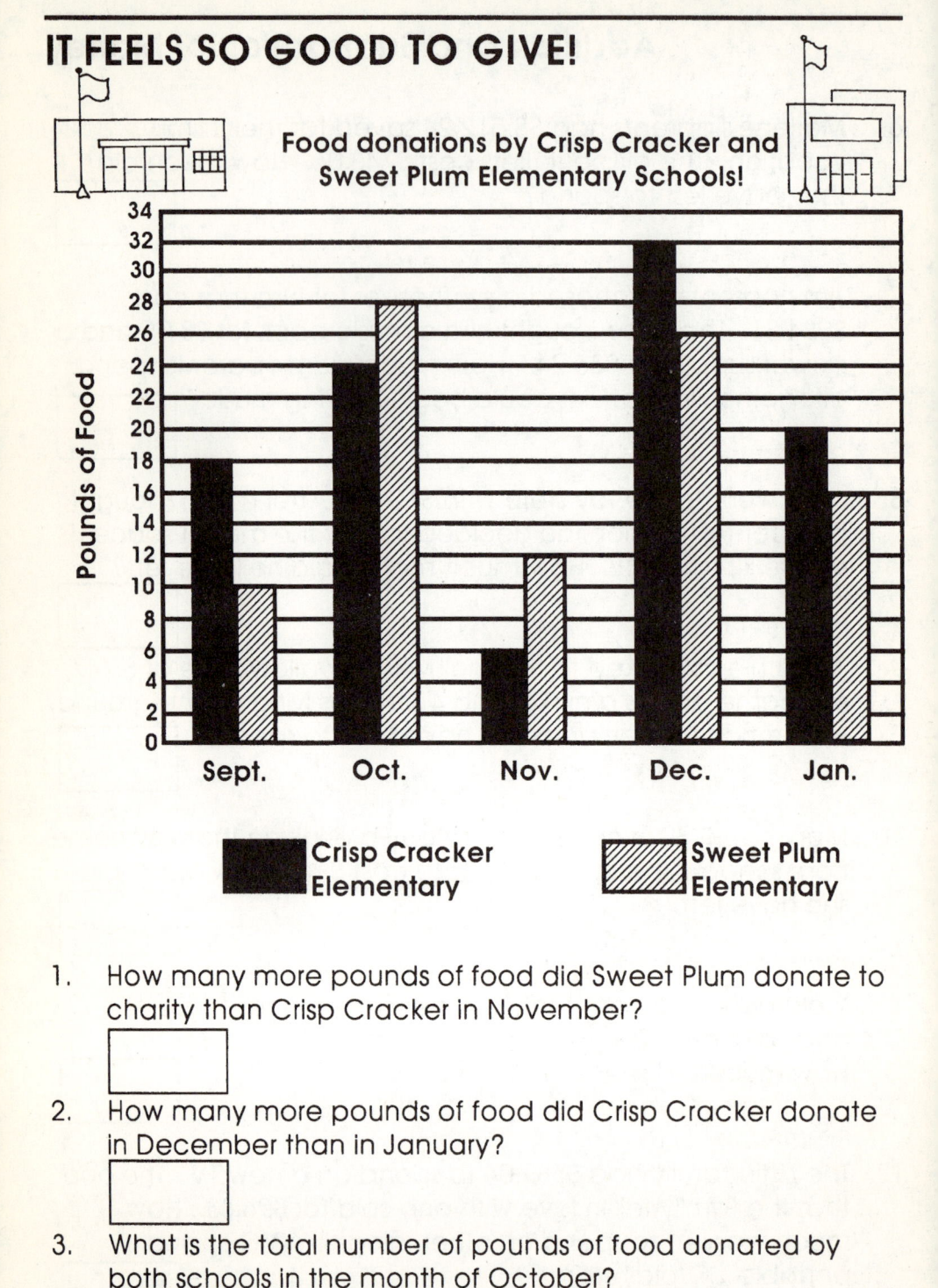

Food donations by Crisp Cracker and Sweet Plum Elementary Schools!

■ Crisp Cracker Elementary

▨ Sweet Plum Elementary

1. How many more pounds of food did Sweet Plum donate to charity than Crisp Cracker in November?

2. How many more pounds of food did Crisp Cracker donate in December than in January?

3. What is the total number of pounds of food donated by both schools in the month of October?

© 2006 Frank Schaffer Publications

Using a Double Bar Graph

4. Which school donated the least amount of food during one month?

5. Which school donated the greatest amount of food during one month?

6. What is the difference between Sweet Plum's greatest month of donations and its least month of donations?

7. What is the total number of pounds of food that the students and faculty at Sweet Plum donated during the first five months of school?

8. What is the average number of pounds of food that Crisp Cracker donated in the first five months of school?

9. List the months of donated food from Sweet Plum, greatest to least.

10. What is the total amount of food that was donated from both schools for the first five months of school?

11. Which school donated more food for the hungry?

12. Which school had the greatest range of donations from two different months?

WHERE DID TIME LEARN TO FLY?

1. Chris arrives at school at 8:25 a.m. He leaves for home at 3:40 p.m. How long is he at school?

2. Last week, Nina spent 480 minutes practicing her flute. How many hours does that equal?

3. Lisa arrived at her friend's house at 11:42 a.m. She stayed for 3 hours. What time did she leave her friend's house?

4. Tom went to the batting cages at 10:45 a.m. He finally got tired at 11:52 a.m. and decided to head home. How long did he practice hitting those line drives and home runs?

5. Linda got paid $2.25 per hour for a total of $6.75 for baby-sitting. She arrived at the home where she was to work at 6:05 p.m. What time did she finish baby-sitting?

Time

6. Curt stayed a total of 53 hours in the bottom of the Grand Canyon. How many days and extra hours was that in all?

7. Clinton spent 3 hours and 25 minutes at the mall watching an action-packed movie and having lunch. He arrived there at 11:05 a.m. What time did he leave?

8. Lynnette and David wanted to call their grandparents in New York. There was a 3-hour time difference. They made their call at 10:27 a.m. If it was later in New York, what time was it when their grandmother answered the phone?

9. Christina's birthday party at the skating rink started at 11:15 a.m. It was over at 2:17 p.m. How long did the party last?

10. Doug arrived at the skateboard demonstrations at 1:10 p.m. They went on for 1 hour and 17 minutes after he arrived. What time did they end?

11. Eva's plane took off at 5:09 p.m. Her flight lasted exactly 2 hours and 18 minutes. What time did her plane land?

12. Alecia was rewarded by her parents with 15 minutes of ice-skating time for each $\frac{1}{2}$ hour of homework that she did during the week. She spent 90 minutes at the skating rink on Saturday. How many hours of homework did she do last week?

THERE ARE SO MANY FUN THINGS TO DO!

1. Charlie zoomed down the special, curved cement path for skateboards a total of 3 times. The length of the path is 1,398 feet. How many feet in all did he glide down the path?

2. The rollerblade course was 6,214 feet long. If Natalie completed it 6 times, how many feet in all did she zoom around the course?

3. Each of the 4 boys on the campout finished the entire orienteering course that was a length of 12,345 steps. How many steps in all did this equal?

4. Each of the 8 children splashed and turned down the 342-foot water slide with a smile the whole way. How many feet did they glide altogether?

5. Both of the pools at the bottom of the water slides were filled with 34,108 gallons of water. How much water is this in all?

Multiplication of Whole Numbers

6. During the pinball game, Richard hit the bar that scores 9 times the present points earned. If Richard had 2,105 points at that time, how many points did he earn when he hit the special bar?

7. Each of the 8 students with kites had 463 feet of string let out into the air. How many feet in all did they have let out?

8. Each of the 5 boys that came to the lake swam all the way across, which was a total of 13,657 feet. How many feet did they swim altogether?

9. Each of the 7 boys and girls that flashed down the sidewalk on their rollerblades continued around town for a total of 5,213 feet before stopping. How many feet did they glide altogether?

10. The track that Earl made for his handlebar skateboard was a total of 8,942 feet. How many feet did he travel if he went around the track 4 times?

11. Each of the 3 jets that the students flew to get to California weighed 58,314 pounds empty. How much did these 3 planes weigh?

12. It took David 3,121 strokes with his paddles to get his canoe completely across the lake. How many strokes would it take him in all to cross the lake 3 times?

DON'T YOU JUST LOVE DOGS?

1. 24 children at Tammy's school own dogs that each weigh 85 pounds! How much do these dogs weigh altogether?

2. A total of 52 children at the dog show brought pets that each weighed in at 131 pounds. How much did these dogs weigh altogether?

3. Lowell discovered that 81 of the students in his school owned dogs that each drank 3,514 gallons of water last year. How many gallons of water does that total in all?

4. 23 dogs were 117 cm long from the tips of their noses to the ends of their tails. How many centimeters does this add up to altogether?

5. Barbara found out that 56 children in the fifth grade each fed their canine chompers 398 pounds of food this year. How much is that altogether?

Multiplication of Whole Numbers

6. Kirk called the Humane Society and found out that in the last 19 years, his city had registered 31,245 dogs each year. How many cuddly tail-waggers is that in all?

7. Madeline discovered that the pet store near her house has made 91 orders of dog food this year. Each order contained 4,124 pounds of food. How many pounds is that in all?

8. Vaudine could not believe that 62 boys and girls from her school owned doggy athletes that could each chase a Frisbee™ for 312 feet and then chomp it down between their teeth and bring it back to their owner without stopping. How many feet does this add up to in all?

9. Diana and Mike put together a 1,005-meter fun run for the dogs in their class to warm up with before their Dog Day began. They had a total of 84 dogs that showed up for the fun. If each of them ran the entire course, what is the total number of meters the dogs ran altogether?

10. 92 of the sniffing canines had snouts that each measured 14 cm in length. How long would this be if these snouts were put together?

11. Eva and David felt that they had the friendliest class of dogs in the world. They calculated that their dogs each wag their tails about 4,251 times every day. If 21 boys and girls own dogs in their class, how many wags is that each day?

COOL OFF AT CAMP IN THE SUMMERTIME!

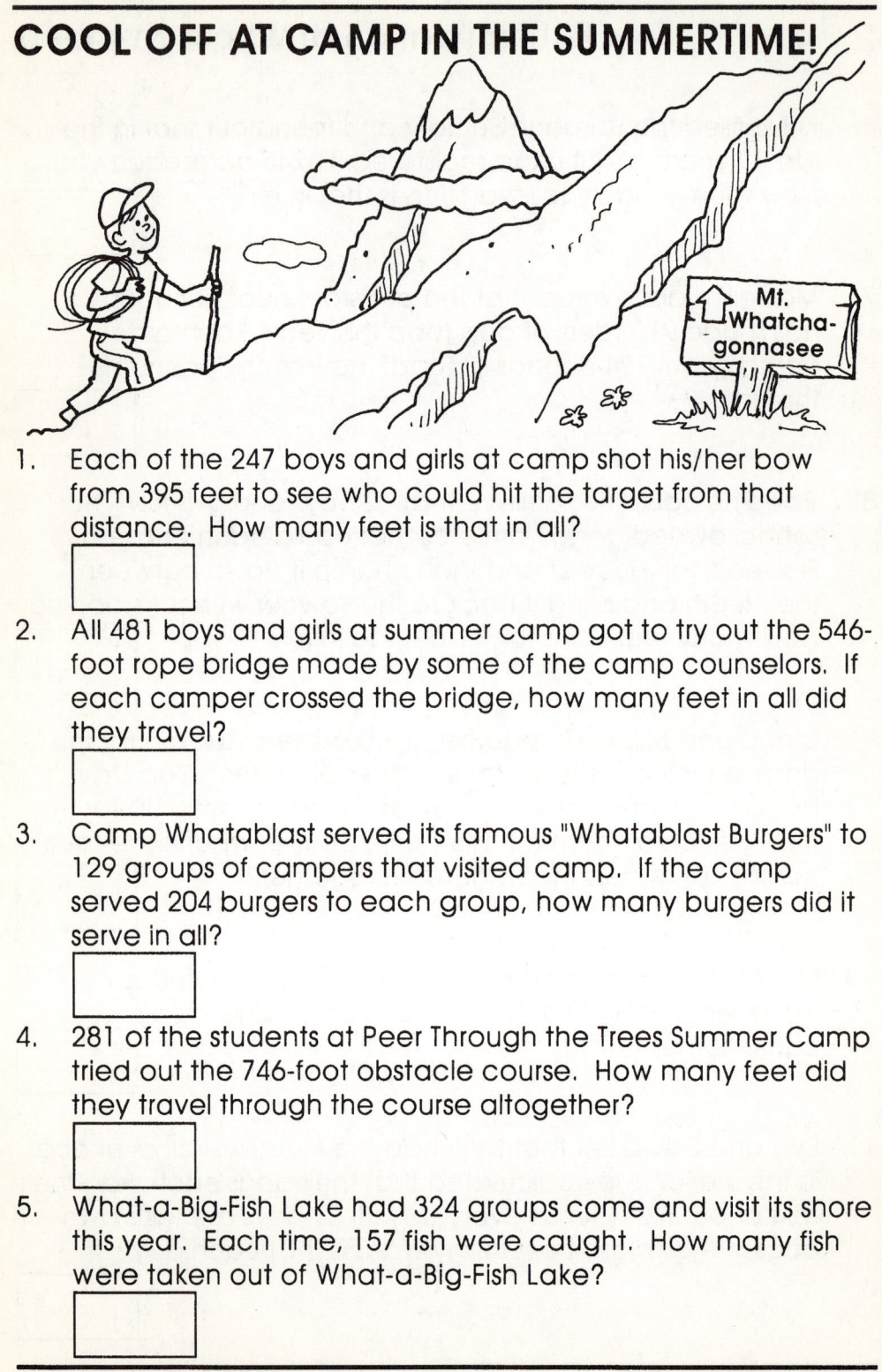

1. Each of the 247 boys and girls at camp shot his/her bow from 395 feet to see who could hit the target from that distance. How many feet is that in all?

2. All 481 boys and girls at summer camp got to try out the 546-foot rope bridge made by some of the camp counselors. If each camper crossed the bridge, how many feet in all did they travel?

3. Camp Whatablast served its famous "Whatablast Burgers" to 129 groups of campers that visited camp. If the camp served 204 burgers to each group, how many burgers did it serve in all?

4. 281 of the students at Peer Through the Trees Summer Camp tried out the 746-foot obstacle course. How many feet did they travel through the course altogether?

5. What-a-Big-Fish Lake had 324 groups come and visit its shore this year. Each time, 157 fish were caught. How many fish were taken out of What-a-Big-Fish Lake?

Multiplication of Whole Numbers

6. Each of the 320 campers was required to spend 819 minutes at camp cleaning up and helping to make it more beautiful. How many minutes is this in all? Do you know about how many hours this would be?

7. During the summer while Camp Let's Make Art was open, a total of 643 boys and girls each wove 295 inches of friendship bracelets and key chain ropes. How many inches did that total?

8. Each of the 421 campers at swim camp cruised back and forth in the pool a total of 564 times during his/her stay. How many laps is that in all?

9. 386 of the campers wanted to climb the 452-meter hike to the top of Mt. Whatchagonnasee. How many meters did they climb in all if each camper made it to the top?

10. 298 happy campers at Camp You're Gonna Have Fun were able to carry an egg on a spoon for a distance of 378 feet without dropping it. How many feet was this in all?

11. 147 of the campers wanted to try out the 389-meter canoe challenge course on the lake. If each camper made it all the way, how many meters did they canoe in all?

12. Using the rope course, 276 campers were able to cross the pond without touching the ground. The course was 267 feet long. How many feet did the campers travel in all crossing the pond?

MONEY REALLY ADDS UP FAST!

Forcipiger longirostris

1. Eight students each bought a pen from the school bookstore that sold for $.93 each. How much did they spend in all?

2. 42 students ordered the exciting new novel the librarian let them know about. Each one sold for $3.95. How much did the order cost altogether?

3. Five scouts ordered the binoculars that were in the wilderness store. They sold for $28.93 each. How much was spent on the binoculars in all?

4. Seven friends went to the amusement park last Saturday to have fun on the famous roller coaster. Tickets for admission were $5.83. What was the total cost of admission?

5. All 35 students in Mr. Kaufman's science class wanted to build a model rocket. If they sold for $8.07 each, what was the total cost of these rocket kits?

© 2006 Frank Schaffer Publications

Multiplication of Money

6. David bought 6 super bouncing balls to share with his friends during recess. They cost $.28 each. How much did he pay in all for the balls?

7. Riverdale Elementary School ordered 231 new math books. Each one sold for $8.93. How much did it pay for this order altogether?

8. After hearing about the incredible name this fish had, 58 students at Mark's school bought a poster with a picture of this fish on it for $.96. How much did they pay in all for these posters?

9. This year, 37 boys and girls each bought aquariums for their pet reptiles at Pete's Animal Supply Center. Each aquarium sold for $46.82. How much have these boys and girls spent in all for homes for their reptiles?

10. A total of 642 boys and girls has come to Totally Toys to purchase the new yo-yo that actually sings when you pull it down to do tricks. Each one sold for $3.76. How much has Totally Toys received from the sales of this yo-yo?

11. All 29 students paid $6.37 to attend the field trip to the amusement park where you get to drive boats around the pond! How much did they pay altogether for admission?

12. All 87 band members paid $4.35 to eat at the kids only buffet restaurant on the way back from their performance. How much did they pay altogether for this exclusive meal?

OH BOY, IT'S TIME FOR A FIELD TRIP!

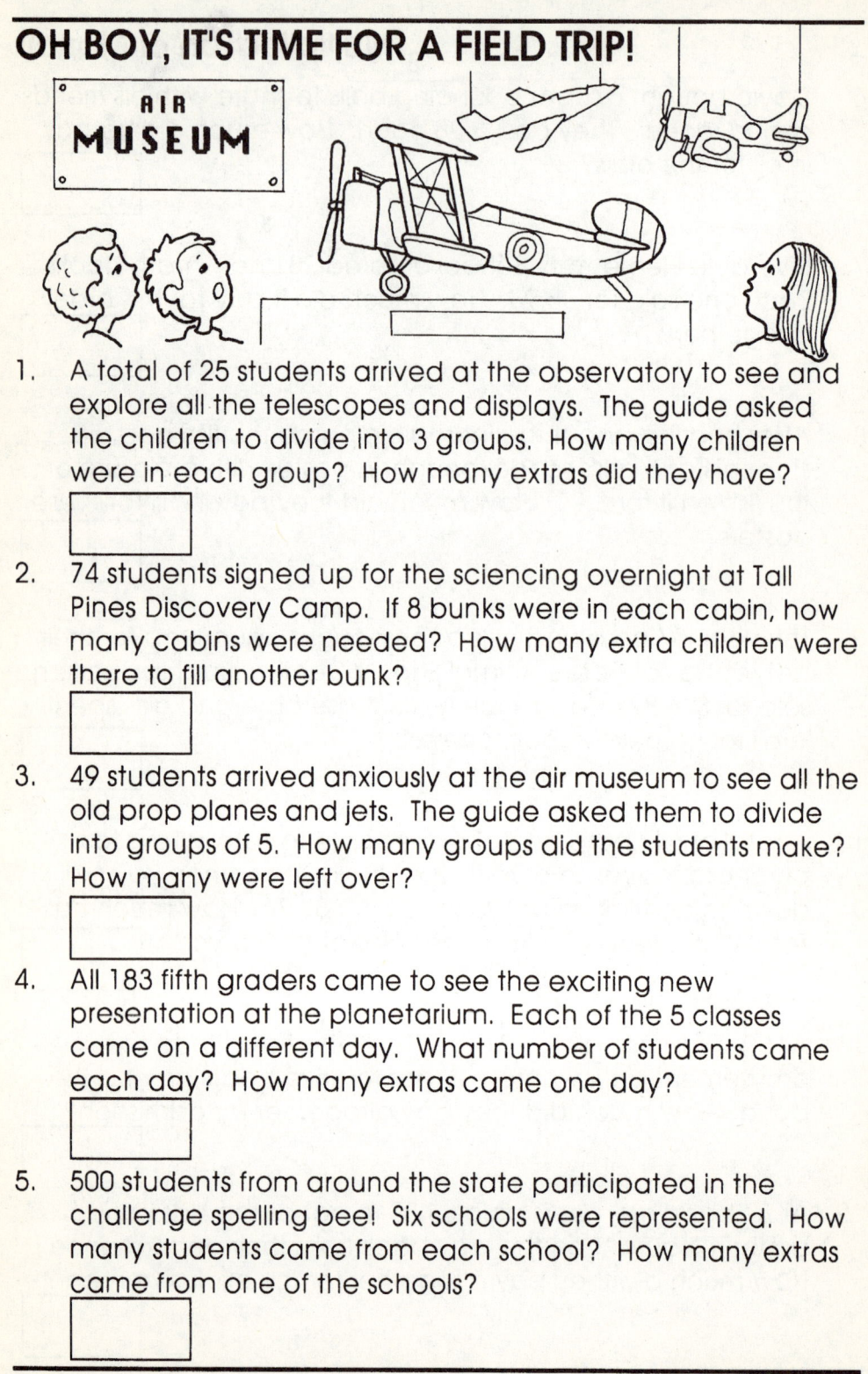

1. A total of 25 students arrived at the observatory to see and explore all the telescopes and displays. The guide asked the children to divide into 3 groups. How many children were in each group? How many extras did they have?

2. 74 students signed up for the sciencing overnight at Tall Pines Discovery Camp. If 8 bunks were in each cabin, how many cabins were needed? How many extra children were there to fill another bunk?

3. 49 students arrived anxiously at the air museum to see all the old prop planes and jets. The guide asked them to divide into groups of 5. How many groups did the students make? How many were left over?

4. All 183 fifth graders came to see the exciting new presentation at the planetarium. Each of the 5 classes came on a different day. What number of students came each day? How many extras came one day?

5. 500 students from around the state participated in the challenge spelling bee! Six schools were represented. How many students came from each school? How many extras came from one of the schools?

Division of Whole Numbers

6. A total of 314 band members from 4 schools attended the statewide band festival held in Yosemite National Park. How many students came from each school? How many extras came from one of the schools?

7. Both fifth grade classes from Reggie's school came on the trip to Sutter's Mill to see where the gold rush started. The director of the museum asked the 60 children to divide into 7 groups. How many students were in each group? How many extras were there?

8. 365 students from 8 schools came to join in on the fossil dig. How many students came from each school? How many extras came from one of the schools?

9. A total of 742 boys and girls representing 9 schools showed up for Beach Day on the last day of school. How many students came from each school? How many extras came?

10. A total of 143 students from 4 classrooms came to be face to face with the exotic animal petting zoo exhibits. How many students came from each classroom, and how many extras did one classroom have?

11. 450 students from Keystone Elementary School came to play in the snow at the ski resort near town. Seven grade levels from the school came along. How many students from each grade level came along, and how many extras were there?

MADE AND DESIGNED 100% BY KIDS!

1. Nine of the students at Cinnamon Elementary School passed out a total of 1,917 flyers to the homes near school telling about the carnival on Saturday! How many flyers did each student pass out?

2. Frisbee™ Elementary School printed its own student newspaper for the kids around town. A total of 2,910 copies were printed to distribute to 6 elementary schools. How many went to each school?

3. Barbara's school decided to give out the button that she designed to remind everyone to keep their city clean. The school printed a total of 1,729 buttons for both elementary schools in her town. How many did each school receive? How many extras were there?

4. Monica was so excited when the local newspaper decided to print her comic strip in its evening edition! After the newspaper printed the first of her comic strips, it printed 2 more. All 3 editions came to a total of 1,958 papers. How many papers were published in each edition? How many extras were printed of one of the editions?

Division of Whole Numbers

5. A total of 1,670 tickets was printed for 7 performances of Rocky Road Elementary School's famous play, "Brocoli Pie!" How many tickets were printed for each performance? How many extras were printed?

6. 4,635 students from 5 elementary schools each submitted a name that the new panda now living in the local city zoo should be called. How many different names did each school submit?

7. Mrs. Chimebell let her student Leon design the invitation for the school science fair. 1,408 invitations were printed and divided evenly among 8 grade levels. How many invitations were distributed to each grade level?

8. A total of 2,728 entries was received from 4 schools for the skateboard/rollerblade rodeo! How many entries were received from each school?

9. 1,924 students from 5 schools sent in a drawing of what they thought the new park downtown should look like. How many sketches came from each school? How many extras were received?

10. The Parks and Recreation Department printed and distributed 5,568 flyers to 6 schools letting the kids around town know about the softball championship and celebration. How many were sent to each school?

© 2006 Frank Schaffer Publications   0-88012-863-1

LET'S GO SEE "AMERICA THE BEAUTIFUL!"

1. A total of 483 students from Monica's school toured Crater Lake National Park. They took 6 buses. How many students were on each bus? How many extra students were on one of the buses?

2. A total of 1,521 boys and girls from 3 schools enjoyed the magnificent caves at Carlsbad Caverns National Park! How many students came from each school?

3. There were 1,210 children from the 2 schools in Bill's town that visited Yosemite National Park in California. How many children from each school went?

4. Eight groups came out to see the glaciers at Glacier National Park in Montana. A total of 567 children enjoyed the trip. How many children were in each group? How many extras were there?

5. During the school year, 9 schools visited Sequoia National Park in California! There were 1,872 students in all that got to see firsthand what a tree about 2,500 years old looks like and what it is like to drive right through the middle of a tree! How many students came from each school?

Division of Whole Numbers

6. 635 girls from Katelyn's scout troop wanted to hike down to see the Grand Canyon for themselves. They divided into 7 groups to make the trip. How many scouts were in each group? How many extras were there?

7. 2,882 children from 3 towns made the trip to see Old Faithful in Yellowstone National Park last summer! How many children went from each town? How many extras were there?

8. 202 boys and girls arrived on 5 buses to hike around and enjoy the Blue Ridge Mountains and the Shenandoah River in Shenandoah National Park. How many children came on each bus? How many were left over?

9. Four groups of hikers went to North Cascades National Park to explore and have fun. A total of 240 boys and girls went. How many hikers were in each group that went to Washington?

10. A total of 1,202 students from 5 schools came to see and explore the animal fossils in Badlands National Park. How many students came from each school to visit this park in South Dakota? How many extra students came from one of the schools?

11. Two groups of students flew to the island of Hawaii to see for themselves what an active volcano looks like! A total of 606 students made the exciting trip! How many students were in each group?

WE HAVE ENGINE IGNITION AND LIFT-OFF!

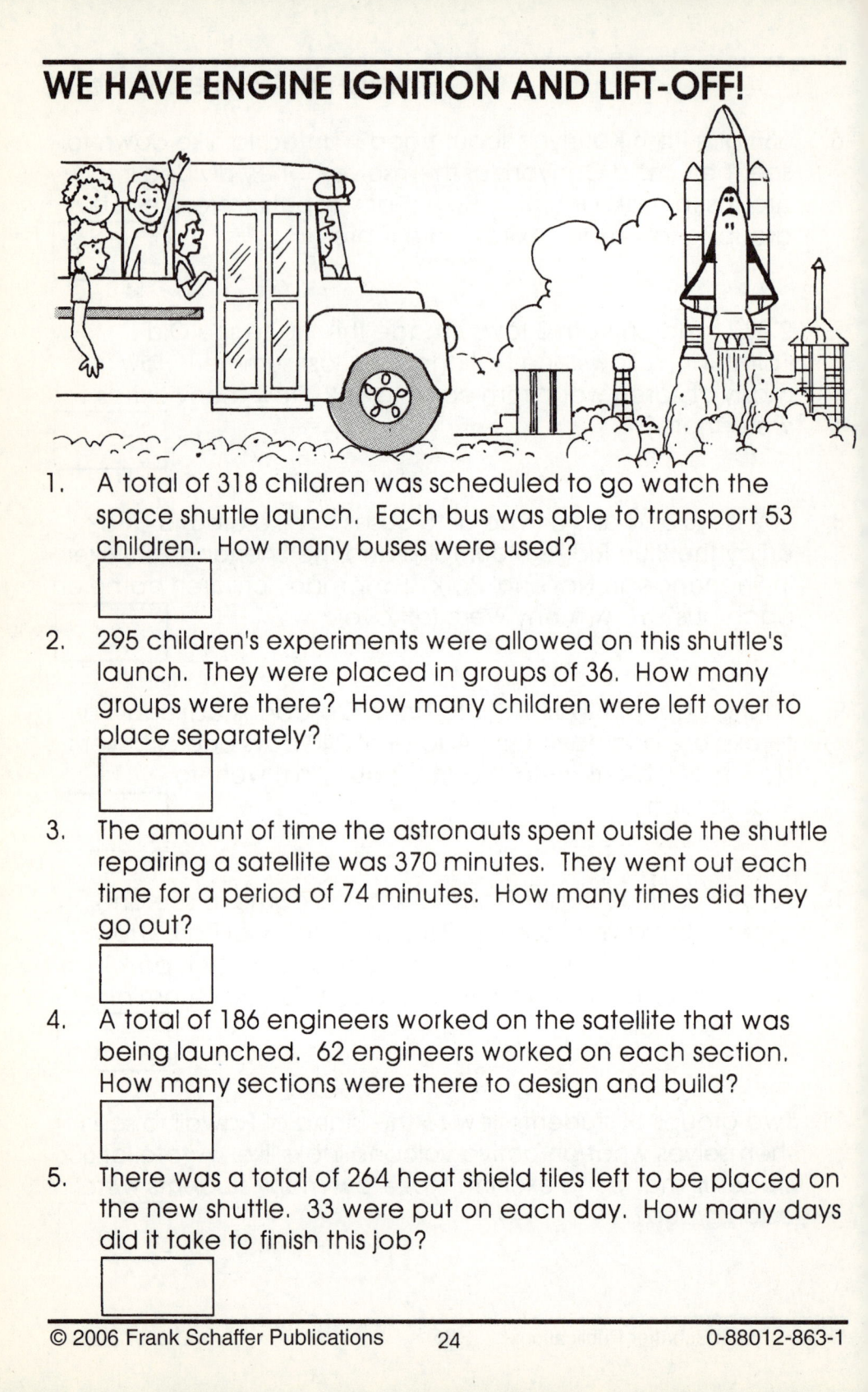

1. A total of 318 children was scheduled to go watch the space shuttle launch. Each bus was able to transport 53 children. How many buses were used?

2. 295 children's experiments were allowed on this shuttle's launch. They were placed in groups of 36. How many groups were there? How many children were left over to place separately?

3. The amount of time the astronauts spent outside the shuttle repairing a satellite was 370 minutes. They went out each time for a period of 74 minutes. How many times did they go out?

4. A total of 186 engineers worked on the satellite that was being launched. 62 engineers worked on each section. How many sections were there to design and build?

5. There was a total of 264 heat shield tiles left to be placed on the new shuttle. 33 were put on each day. How many days did it take to finish this job?

Division of Whole Numbers

6. There was a total of 192 hours until lift-off of *Discovery*. How many days were left until the launch?

7. On one of the flights, a new course had to be made, and the engines burned for a total of 221 seconds. Each burning was a period of 65 seconds. How many times were the engines ignited? How many extra seconds did the engines burn on one of the ignitions?

8. All 736 children sat around television monitors at Raleigh's school to watch the space shuttle *Discovery* launch into space! 92 children were huddled around each monitor. How many monitors did they have to view from?

9. There were 220 students in all that attended Space Camp during the summer! Each group had 41 boys and girls. How many groups met during the summer? How many extra students were in one group?

10. 174 people were seated in 87 cars along the road to watch the shuttle land. How many people were in each car?

11. A total of 90 students wanted to learn how to become astronauts. 21 students from each classroom wanted to send away for a list of training qualifications. How many classrooms were interested? How many extra students were in one of the classrooms?

THERE'S LEARNING OUTSIDE THE CLASSROOM TOO!

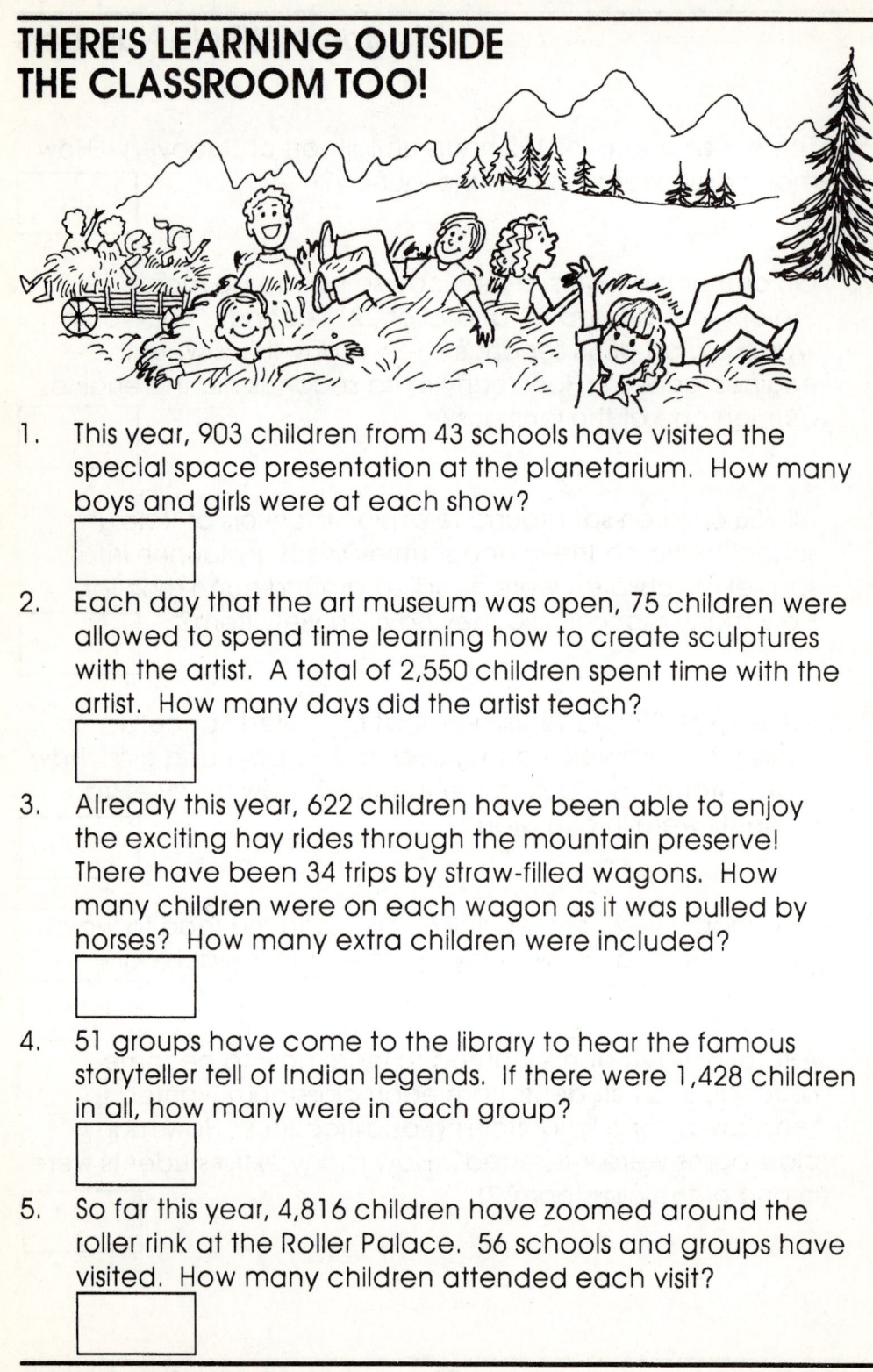

1. This year, 903 children from 43 schools have visited the special space presentation at the planetarium. How many boys and girls were at each show?

2. Each day that the art museum was open, 75 children were allowed to spend time learning how to create sculptures with the artist. A total of 2,550 children spent time with the artist. How many days did the artist teach?

3. Already this year, 622 children have been able to enjoy the exciting hay rides through the mountain preserve! There have been 34 trips by straw-filled wagons. How many children were on each wagon as it was pulled by horses? How many extra children were included?

4. 51 groups have come to the library to hear the famous storyteller tell of Indian legends. If there were 1,428 children in all, how many were in each group?

5. So far this year, 4,816 children have zoomed around the roller rink at the Roller Palace. 56 schools and groups have visited. How many children attended each visit?

Division of Whole Numbers

6. 1,549 students from 28 schools had visited George Washington's house and tomb in Mount Vernon, Virginia, when Eva's class arrived. How many students were from each school? How many extras were from one of the schools?

7. Last year, 91 classes visited Meteor Crater to see the gigantic hole left by the impact of the meteorite. A total of 3,276 children came in all! How many children came on each visit?

8. 889 students from 22 schools have visited the Mineral Museum this year! How many students have attended from each school? How many extras have there been?

9. The local dairy has had 56 visits by schools in the area. A total of 4,622 students has come to learn about the production of milk and other dairy products. How many students have attended on each visit? How many extras have there been?

10. 861 students from 31 schools have come to see the ancient Indian ruins on the side of the mountain near town. How many students have attended each visit? How many extras have attended?

11. In the first three months of this year, 1,262 students from 47 classrooms have visited Niagara Falls in New York! How many students have visited on each trip? How many extras have attended?

BUSINESS IS BOOMING TODAY!

1. When Merrill's Market advertised its 2-foot long cucumbers on sale, 8,733 of them were sold in 41 days. How many were sold each day?

2. Buford's Burger Buffet sold 4,978 "big burgers" in 35 days. How many did it sell each day? How many extras did it sell?

3. Kathy's Clothing Closet could not believe the response from its newspaper and television ads. The store sold 15,210 pairs of its mouse shoes in 90 days. How many did it sell each day?

4. Romelia's Roasted and Ready Restaurant sold 6,345 of its world famous boiled bags of peanuts in 15 days! How many bags did it sell each day?

5. Mitchell's Microphone Mart sold 11,392 of its new slimline, wireless microphones in 64 days. The store found out that magazine advertising is just right for it. How many mikes did it sell each day?

Division of Whole Numbers

6. Harry's Handyman Service received 9,792 calls in just 73 days. The phone was ringing off the wall! How many calls did it receive each day requesting work to be done? How many extra calls did it get?

7. Kelly's Corn Dog Stand sold 8,324 of its delectable dogs in the first 23 days of business. How many of these delicious dogs did the stand sell each day? How many extras did it sell?

8. Pete's Pipes and Sprinklers sold 8,500 pieces in just 32 days after putting up its new neon sign. How many pieces of pipe and such did it sell each day? How many extra pieces did it sell?

9. Stanley's Skateboard Stopover sold 5,838 really cool stickers that read, "I'm a Zoomer!" in just 14 days. The store couldn't believe the response! How many stickers did it sell each day?

10. Felipe's Fence Factory just finished selling 7,987 fence posts in just 58 days! Certainly the beautiful fence that the company put around its store made a big difference! How many posts did it sell each day? How many extras did it sell?

11. David's Doorknob Directory helped 8,431 customers find the right doorknob for them in just 16 days. It was delightfully distracted by all the calls! How many customers did the service help each day? How many extras did it serve?

CLUBS ARE SO MUCH FUN!

1. All 7 members of the recyclable club found enough cans to earn $6.02 on their first trip cleaning up! How much money did each member earn?

2. The 8-member rollerblade club happened upon an old purse with no identification. Inside was $13.76. How much did each member get if it was divided evenly?

3. While biking through the park, David and John kept cool by each bringing along a drink. They paid a total of $1.78 for these thirst quenchers. How much did each drink cost?

4. All 39 members of the band received a ribbon to wear to show their school spirit during the faculty football game. The total cost was $32.76. How much did each ribbon cost?

5. Mr. Kliklouder paid a total of $16.91 to buy all 19 members of the science club a special neon pencil that tells the temperature in Celsius degrees. How much did he pay for each pen?

© 2006 Frank Schaffer Publications

Division of Money

6. Theresa paid a total of $2.56 to buy 4 huge bones from the butcher to cook and give to her pooch to chew on while she did her homework. What was the price of each bone?

7. For the first hour of the car wash, 6 scrubbers and polishers of the student council brought in a total of $16.74 in donations for their school. How much does that equal in earnings for each worker?

8. All 16 members of the math club bought a baseball cap with the club's special logo on it. The members paid a total of $12.96. How much did each baseball cap cost?

9. Nine students from Jolie's class ordered a special *What's Wrong With This Picture?* book. The order came to a total of $32.04. How much did each book cost?

10. Gabriel spent a total of $3.45 to buy herself and 4 other friends school spirit buttons. How much did she pay for each button?

11. The fifth grade teachers bought a total of 56 treats for the students to enjoy during the special drama presentation. They paid a total of $37.52. What was the cost of each treat?

12. Mrs. Moore ordered special pencils for her class that read, "You're Doing a Great Job!" She ordered 35 pencils for a total cost of $9.45. How much did she pay for each pencil?

DECIMALS CAN BE SIMPLY DELIGHTFUL!

1. Jeff's mom was planning the most delicious salad that he would ever eat. She purchased 0.92 kg of snow peas, 1.3 kg of juicy, ripe tomatoes and 4.243 kg of jicama. How many kilograms of vegetables did she buy in all?

2. Cyndi decided to build a birdhouse and other woodworking projects. She went to the store and bought 3.06 kg of long nails, 0.8 kg of finishing nails and 29.76 kg of all different types of wood. What was the total weight of her purchase?

3. Michelle purchased 861.24 g of whole wheat flour and 289.19 g of cornmeal to make her famous corn muffins! How many grams of flour and cornmeal did she buy in all?

4. Al's science experiment called for 6.01 mL of vinegar and 3.14 mL of water. How many more milliliters of vinegar did he need?

5. In one of the boxes of books in Kelly's room were 43.203 kg of comic books. That's a lot of comics! She took out 12.419 kg of them so that she could try to lift the box. How much did the box of comics weigh after she took some out?

Decimals

6. Eva put 6,214.3 L of water into her backyard pool. After splashing and jumping with her friends all day long, 1,821.9 L of water was knocked out. How many liters of water was left in the pool at the end of the day?

7. Each of the 5 sets of rollerblades weighed 8.93 kg. How much did they weigh in all?

8. Four of the dogs that the students in Monica's class own weigh 41.2 kg each. How many kilograms is this?

9. At David's school, an average of 1.29 days each year there are 18.3 children absent. How many absences is this in all?

10. Both cages from the school science lab weighed 7.3 kg. How many kilograms did each of them weigh?

11. As a math activity in Tom's class, the teacher asked him to weigh all 27 booklets. He found out that they weighed 16.2 kg altogether. What was the weight of each booklet?

12. Deborah found out that the pile of 42 paper clips she had weighed 26.46 g. What was the weight of each paper clip?

FRACTIONS DO ADD UP!

1. At Sonja's birthday party, $\frac{5}{10}$ of her birthday cake was served to her friends. Another $\frac{3}{10}$ was enjoyed by her family when she got home. What fraction of her cake was eaten?

2. During Samuel's sleepover, $\frac{8}{16}$ of the power in his batteries was used. Another $\frac{3}{16}$ of the power was used when he practiced his new skit for the talent show. What fraction of the power was used?

3. Virginia spent $\frac{1}{7}$ of her allowance on fancy pencils for school. She spent another $\frac{4}{7}$ of her allowance to go to the movies. What fraction of her allowance has she spent so far?

4. During Kite Day at school, $\frac{8}{21}$ of Richard's class wanted to fly box kites. Another $\frac{7}{21}$ of his class wanted to fly regular trapezoid-shaped kites. What fraction of his class wanted to fly kites?

5. In January, $\frac{3}{9}$ of the animals at the Humane Society were cats. In February, $\frac{4}{9}$ of the animals were little meowers! What was the total fraction of cats at the Humane Society during these two months?

© 2006 Frank Schaffer Publications

Addition of Fractions

6. During the first half of the soccer game, $\frac{7}{15}$ of Andy's kicks were right on target. During the second half, another $\frac{7}{15}$ of his kicks put the ball right where he wanted it. What fraction of his kicking was right on target during the game?

7. Sophia nibbled on $\frac{2}{11}$ of her apple during lunch. After school, she discovered that she had saved it in her lunch box and nibbled on another $\frac{5}{11}$ of it! What fraction of her apple had Sophia eaten in all?

8. In Vaughn's class, $\frac{14}{30}$ of the students finished their state reports before they were due on Friday. An additional $\frac{7}{30}$ of her class completed them on Friday. What fraction of the students in her class got the reports finished on time?

9. At Anna's school, $\frac{10}{20}$ of the students ordered fried chicken on Wednesday for lunch. Another $\frac{7}{20}$ of the students ordered hamburgers. What fraction of the students ordered lunch?

10. Rebecca gave her puppy $\frac{7}{24}$ of the doggy biscuits in the box the first day she bought them. Boy, was her little tail-wagger happy! During the rest of the week, she gave him another $\frac{14}{24}$ of the biscuits. What fraction of the box has the cute, little puppy eaten so far?

11. When Matthew arrived to have fun at the city pool, $\frac{2}{5}$ of it was being used! While he was there, another $\frac{1}{5}$ of the pool filled up. What fraction of the pool was being used while Matthew was swimming?

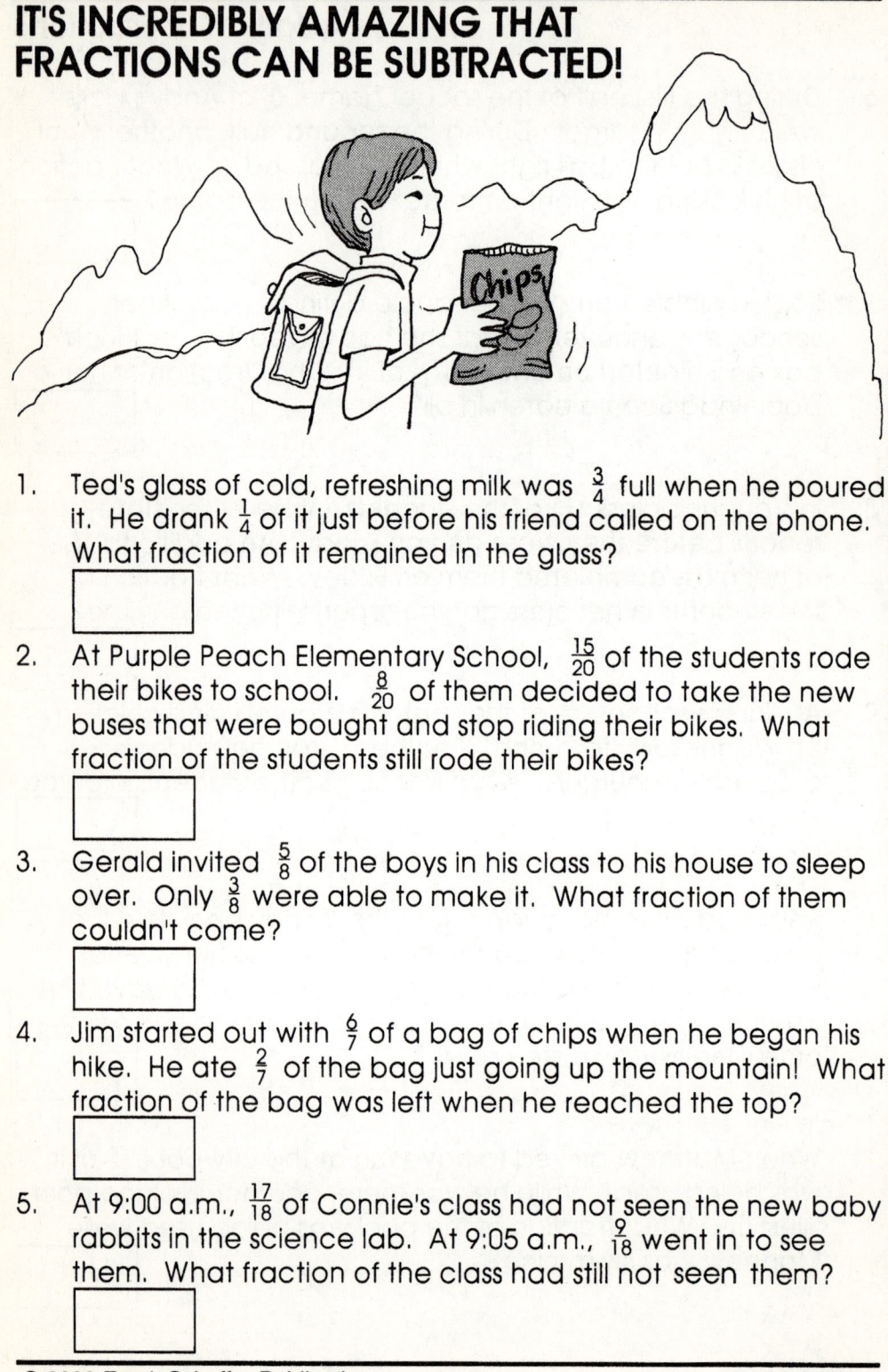

IT'S INCREDIBLY AMAZING THAT FRACTIONS CAN BE SUBTRACTED!

1. Ted's glass of cold, refreshing milk was $\frac{3}{4}$ full when he poured it. He drank $\frac{1}{4}$ of it just before his friend called on the phone. What fraction of it remained in the glass?

2. At Purple Peach Elementary School, $\frac{15}{20}$ of the students rode their bikes to school. $\frac{8}{20}$ of them decided to take the new buses that were bought and stop riding their bikes. What fraction of the students still rode their bikes?

3. Gerald invited $\frac{5}{8}$ of the boys in his class to his house to sleep over. Only $\frac{3}{8}$ were able to make it. What fraction of them couldn't come?

4. Jim started out with $\frac{6}{7}$ of a bag of chips when he began his hike. He ate $\frac{2}{7}$ of the bag just going up the mountain! What fraction of the bag was left when he reached the top?

5. At 9:00 a.m., $\frac{17}{18}$ of Connie's class had not seen the new baby rabbits in the science lab. At 9:05 a.m., $\frac{9}{18}$ went in to see them. What fraction of the class had still not seen them?

© 2006 Frank Schaffer Publications

Tutor's Guide

This Tutor's Guide contains answer keys for Math Word Problems - Grade 5. Pull it out from the book to use as a guide.

INTERESTING SCHOOL FACTS!

1. 385 words were on the spelling bee study sheet. 929 words were added just to help students learn any words that might prove to be really tough. How many words were there in all to study?
   1314

2. The students at Colored Leaf Elementary School wrote adjectives to describe their school. The words, when put side by side, measured 601 inches in length. The sign on the front of the school only measures 314 inches. How much longer are the adjectives than the sign on the front of the school?
   287

3. A total of 407 pens was ordered for the whole year at Green Trails Elementary School. After 4 months, 189 pens were used. How many pens are left for the rest of the year?
   218

4. Antie Creek Elementary School used 84,251 sheets of paper in its copier the first half of the school year. It has already used another 29,868 sheets of paper. How many copies has the school made so far this year?
   114119

5. The art teacher used 386 crayons this year. The classroom teachers have used 4,927 sheets of construction paper and 2,134 sheets of writing paper. How many crayons and sheets of paper have the teachers used altogether?
   7447

Addition and Subtraction of Whole Numbers

6. During the hot months, the students at Corn Cob Elementary School drink 6,242 gallons of water. During the cold months, they only drink 3,891 gallons. How many more gallons of water do they drink during the hot months?
   2351

7. Stuart learned that his school used 83,203 sheets of notebook paper this year. He also found out that his school used 12,419 sheets of drawing paper. How many more sheets of notebook paper were used?
   70784

8. The cafeteria ordered 9,234 packets of ketchup, 1,328 pints of orange juice and 3,845 pints of milk. What was the total number of items that the cafeteria ordered?
   14407

9. Rose Elementary School is in a city with a population of 592,840. The neighboring city, which always challenges Rose in the statewide band festivals, has a population of 239,284. How many more people live in the city where Rose Elementary School is located?
   353,556

10. 132,578 students go to school in Jack's town, and 324,954 students go to school in Terry's town. What is the total number of students?
    457,532

11. To build the new multi-purpose room, 234,846 bricks were delivered. To build the cafeteria, only 97,256 bricks were brought in. How many more bricks were delivered to build the multi-purpose room?
    137,590

DO YOU SPEND WISELY?

1. Cheryl had $438.60 in her savings account when she arrived at her bank. She deposited $29.81. How much does she now have in savings?
   $468.41

2. Heather bought a pair of fancy tennis shoes for $51.88. She also purchased a pair of pants for an additional $63.93. How much did she spend in all?
   $115.81

3. Gwen bought a cassette of her favorite music artist for $8.47, lunch for $3.84 and a fancy pen that writes in 4 colors for $.95. How much did she spend in all?
   $13.26

4. Jim and Roger went to the hobby store with $37.06. They found the exact radio-controlled boat they wanted for $28.47. How much money did they have left?
   $8.59

5. Earl had $500.09 in his savings account at the credit union. His parents thought it was a great idea to withdraw $28.76 to purchase the used electric guitar that he saw in the music store window. How much did he have remaining in his savings account?
   $471.33

Addition and Subtraction of Money

6. Marlene's parents had $8,512.24 saved for their family vacation. The airline tickets cost $743.06. How much did they have left to spend?
   $7,769.18

7. Jim's parents purchased a synthesizer for him that cost $924.31. They also bought him a music book for $8.95 and a power supply for $36.24. How much did his parents spend altogether so that Jim could begin making music?
   $969.50

8. Jake went to the toy store with $60.42. After much thought and contemplation, he decided to buy the model space shuttle kit for $9.38. How much money did he have left?
   $51.04

9. As Kathleen walked to the mall with her allowance of $6.47, she came across a nickel and 4 pennies lying on the ground. How much money does she have now to spend?
   $6.56

10. Mary had $.89 in her pocket to buy a drink on the way home from school. The drink she chose cost $.43. How much did she have left?
    $.46

11. Viola bought a comb for $.84, neon shoelaces for $2.47 and, with her parents permission, a new bike for $64.39. How much did she spend in all?
    $67.70

12. The Little family had $589.04 to spend on a new TV. The one that the family fell in love with only sold for $96.83. How much was left to spend on other things like VCR's and portable CD players?
    $492.21

IT FEELS SO GOOD TO GIVE!

Food donations by Crisp Cracker and Sweet Plum Elementary Schools!

1. How many more pounds of food did Sweet Plum donate to charity than Crisp Cracker in November?
   6

2. How many more pounds of food did Crisp Cracker donate in December than in January?
   12

3. What is the total number of pounds of food donated by both schools in the month of October?
   52

Using a Double Bar Graph

4. Which school donated the least amount of food during one month?
   CC Nov

5. Which school donated the greatest amount of food during one month?
   CC Dec

6. What is the difference between Sweet Plum's greatest month of donations and its least month of donations?
   18

7. What is the total number of pounds of food that the students and faculty at Sweet Plum donated during the first five months of school?
   92

8. What is the average number of pounds of food that Crisp Cracker donated in the first five months of school?
   20

9. List the months of donated food from Sweet Plum greatest to least.
   O, D, J, N, S

10. What is the total amount of food that was donated from both schools for the first five months of school?
    192

11. Which school donated more food to the hungry?
    CC

12. Which school had the greatest range of donations from two different months?
    CC

WHERE DID TIME LEARN TO FLY?

1. Chris arrives at school at 8:25 a.m. He leaves for home at 3:40 p.m. How long is he at school?
   7h 15m

2. Last week, Nina spent 480 minutes practicing her flute. How many hours does that equal?
   8h

3. Lisa arrived at her friend's house at 11:42 a.m. She stayed for 3 hours. What time did she leave her friend's house?
   2:42

4. Tom went to the batting cages at 10:45 a.m. He finally got tired at 11:52 a.m. and decided to head home. How long did he practice hitting those line drives and home runs?
   1h 7m

5. Linda got paid $2.25 per hour for a total of $6.75 for baby-sitting. She arrived at the home where she was to work at 6:05 p.m. What time did she finish baby-sitting?
   9:05 pm

© 2006 Frank Schaffer Publications   A   0-88012-863-1

Time

6. Curt stayed a total of 53 hours in the bottom of the Grand Canyon. How many days and extra hours was that in all? **2d 5h**

7. Clinton spent 3 hours and 25 minutes at the mall watching an action-packed movie and having lunch. He arrived there at 11:05 a.m. What time did he leave? **2:30pm**

8. Lynnette and David wanted to call their grandparents in New York. They made their call at 10:27 a.m. If it was later in New York, what time was it when their grandmother answered the phone? **1:27am**

9. Christina's birthday party at the skating rink started at 11:15 a.m. It was over at 2:17 p.m. How long did the party last? **3h 2m**

10. Doug arrived at the skateboard demonstrations at 1:10 p.m. They went on for 1 hour and 17 minutes after he arrived. What time did they end? **2:27pm**

11. Eva's plane took off at 5:09 p.m. Her flight lasted exactly 2 hours and 18 minutes. What time did her plane land? **7:27pm**

12. Alecia was rewarded by her parents with 15 minutes of ice-skating time for each 1 hour of homework that she did during the week. She spent 90 minutes at the skating rink on Tuesday. How many hours of homework did she do last week? **3h**

THERE ARE SO MANY FUN THINGS TO DO!

1. Charlie zoomed down the special, curved cement path for skateboards a total of 3 times. The length of the path is 1,398 feet. How many feet in all did he glide down the path? **4194**

2. The rollerblade course was 6,214 feet long. If Natalie completed it 6 times, how many feet in all did she zoom around the course? **37,284**

3. Each of the 4 boys on the campout finished the entire orienteering course that was a length of 12,345 steps. How many steps in all did this equal? **49,380**

4. Each of the 8 children splashed and turned down the 342-foot water slide with a smile the whole way. How many feet did they glide altogether? **2736**

5. Both of the pools at the bottom of the water slides were filled with 34,108 gallons of water. How much water is this in all? **68,216**

Multiplication of Whole Numbers

6. During the pinball game, Richard hit the bar that scores 9 times the present points earned. If Richard had 2,105 points at that time, how many points did he earn when he hit the special bar? **18,945**

7. Each of the 8 students with kites had 463 feet of string let out into the air. How many feet in all did they have let out? **3704**

8. Each of the 5 boys that came to the lake swam all the way across, which was a total of 13,657 feet. How many feet did they swim altogether? **68,285**

9. Each of the 7 boys and girls that flashed down the sidewalk on their rollerblades continued around town for a total of 5,213 feet before stopping. How many feet did they glide altogether? **34,491**

10. The track that Earl made for his handlebar skateboard was a total of 8,942 feet. How many feet did he travel if he went around the track 4 times? **35,768**

11. Each of the 3 jets that the students flew to get to California weighed 58,314 pounds empty. How much did the 3 planes weigh? **174,942**

12. It took David 3,121 strokes with his paddles to get his canoe completely across the lake. How many strokes would it take him in all to cross the lake 3 times? **9363**

DON'T YOU JUST LOVE DOGS?

1. 24 children at Tommy's school own dogs that each weigh 85 pounds. How much do these dogs weigh altogether? **2040**

2. A total of 52 children at the dog show brought pets that each weighed in at 131 pounds. How much did these dogs weigh altogether? **682**

3. Lowell discovered that 81 of the students in his school owned dogs that each drank 3,514 gallons of water last year. How many gallons of water does that total in all? **284,634**

4. 23 dogs were 117 cm long from the tips of their noses to the ends of their tails. How many centimeters does this add up to altogether? **2691**

5. Barbara found out that 56 children in the fifth grade each fed their canine chompers 398 pounds of food this year. How much is that altogether? **22,288**

Multiplication of Whole Numbers

6. Kirk called the Humane Society and found out that in the last 19 years, his city had registered 31,245 dogs each year. How many cuddly tail-waggers is that in all? **593,655**

7. Madeline discovered that the pet store near her house has made 91 orders of dog food this year. Each order contained 4,124 pounds of food. How many pounds is that in all? **375,284**

8. Vaudine could not believe that 62 boys and girls from her school owned doggy athletes that could chase a Frisbee™ for 312 feet and then chomp it down between their teeth and bring it back to their owner without stopping. How many feet does this add up to in all? **19,344**

9. Diana and Mike put together a 1,005-meter fun run for the dogs in their class to warm up with before their Dog Day began. They had a total of 84 dogs that showed up to the fun. If each of them ran the entire course, what is the total number of meters the dogs ran altogether? **84,420**

10. 92 of the sniffing canines had snouts that each measured 14 cm in length. How long would this be if these snouts were put together? **1288**

11. Eva and David felt that they had the friendliest class of dogs in the world. They calculated that their dogs each wag their tails about 4,251 times every day. If 21 boys and girls own dogs in his class, how many wags is that each day? **89,271**

COOL OFF AT CAMP IN THE SUMMERTIME!

1. Each of the 247 boys and girls at camp shot his/her bow from 395 feet to see who could hit the target from that distance. How many feet is that in all? **97565**

2. All 481 boys and girls at summer camp got to try out the 546-foot rope bridge made by some of the camp counselors. If each camper crossed the bridge, how many feet in all did they travel? **262,626**

3. Camp Whatablast served its famous "Whatablast Burgers" to 129 groups of campers that visited camp. The camp served 204 burgers to each group. How many burgers in all did it serve? **26,316**

4. 281 of the students at Peer Through the Trees Summer Camp tried out the 746-foot obstacle course. How many feet did they travel through the course altogether? **209,626**

5. What a Big-Fish Lake had 324 groups come and visit its shore this year. Each time, 157 fish were caught. How many fish were taken out of What-a-Big-Fish Lake? **50,868**

Multiplication of Whole Numbers

6. Each of the 320 campers was required to spend 819 minutes at camp cleaning up and helping to make it more beautiful. How many minutes is this in all? Do you know about how many hours this would be? **262080 4368**

7. During the annual white Camp Let's Make Art was open, a total of 643 boys and girls each wove 295 inches of friendship bracelets and key chain ropes. How many inches did that total? **189,685**

8. Each of the 421 campers at swim camp cruised back and forth in the pool a total of 564 times during his/her stay. How many laps is that in all? **237,444**

9. 386 of the campers wanted to climb the 452 meter hike to the top of Mt. Whatchagonnasee. How many meters did they climb in all if each camper made it to the top? **174,472**

10. 298 happy campers at Camp You're Gonna Have Fun were able to carry an egg on a spoon for a distance of 378 feet without dropping it. How many feet was this in all? **112,644**

11. 147 of the campers wanted to try out the 389-meter canoe challenge course on the lake. If each camper made it all the way, how many meters did his canoe in all? **57,183**

12. Using the rope course, 276 campers were able to cross the pond without touching the ground. The course was 267 feet long. How many feet did the campers travel in all crossing the pond? **73,692**

MONEY REALLY ADDS UP FAST!

1. Eight students each bought a pen from the school bookstore that sold for $.93 each. How much did they spend in all? **$7.44**

2. 42 students ordered the exciting new novel the librarian let them know about. Each one sold for $3.95. How much did the order cost altogether? **$165.90**

3. Five scouts ordered the binoculars that were in the wilderness store. They sold for $28.93 each. How much was spent on the binoculars in all? **$144.65**

4. Seven friends went to the amusement park last Saturday to have fun on the famous roller coaster. Tickets for admission were $5.83. What was the total cost of admission? **$40.81**

5. All 35 students in Mr. Kaufman's science class wanted to build a model rocket. If they sold for $8.07 each, what was the total cost of these rocket kits? **$282.45**

Multiplication of Money

6. David bought 6 super bouncing balls to share with his friends during recess. They cost $.28 each. How much did he pay in all for the balls? **$1.68**

7. Riverdale Elementary School ordered 231 new math books. Each one sold for $8.93. How much did it pay for this order altogether? **$2062.83**

8. After hearing about the incredible name this fish had, 58 students at Mark's school bought a poster with a picture of this fish on it for $.96. How much did they pay in all for these posters? **$55.68**

9. This year, 37 boys and girls each bought aquariums for their pet reptiles at Pete's Animal Supply Center. Each aquarium sold for $46.82. How much have these boys and girls spent in all for new homes for their reptiles? **$1732.34**

10. A total of 642 boys and girls have come to Totally Toys to purchase the new yo-yo that actually sings when you pull it down to do tricks. Each one sold for $3.76. How much has Totally Toys received from the sales of this yo-yo? **$2413.92**

11. All 29 students paid $6.37 to attend the field trip to the amusement park where you got to drive boats around the pond! How much did they pay altogether for admission? **$184.73**

12. All 87 band members paid $4.35 to eat at the all you can eat buffet restaurant on the way back from their performance. How much did they pay altogether for this exclusive meal? **$378.45**

OH BOY, IT'S TIME FOR A FIELD TRIP!

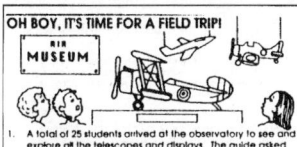

1. A total of 25 students arrived at the observatory to see and explore all the telescopes and displays. The guide asked the children to divide into 3 groups. How many children were in each group? How many extras did they have?
8, 1

2. 74 students signed up for the sciencing overnight at Tall Pines Discovery Camp. If 8 bunks were in each cabin, how many cabins were needed? How many extra children were there to fill another bunk?
9, 2

3. 49 students arrived anxiously at the air museum to see all the old prop planes and jets. The guide asked them to divide into groups of 5. How many groups did the students make? How many were left over?
9, 4

4. All 183 fifth graders came to see the exciting new presentation at the planetarium. Each of the 5 classes came on a different day. What number of students came each day? How many extras came one day?
36, 3

5. 500 students from around the state participated in the challenge spelling bee! Six schools were represented. How many students came from each school? How many extras came from one of the schools?
83, 2

Division of Whole Numbers

6. A total of 314 band members from 4 schools attended the statewide band festival held in Yosemite National Park. How many students came from each school? How many extras came from one of the schools?
78, 2

7. Both fifth grade classes from Reggie's school came on the trip to Sutter's Mill to see where the gold rush started. The director of the museum asked the 60 children to divide into 7 groups. How many students were in each group? How many extras were there?
8, 4

8. 365 students from 8 schools came to join in on the fossil dig. How many students came from each school? How many extras came from one school?
45, 5

9. A total of 742 boys and girls representing 9 schools showed up for Beach Day on the last day of school. How many students came from each school? How many extras came?
82, 4

10. A total of 143 students from 4 classrooms came to be face to face with the exotic animal petting zoo exhibits. How many students came from each classroom, and how many extras did one classroom have?
35, 3

11. 450 students from Keystone Elementary School came to play in the snow at the ski resort near town. Seven grade levels from the school came along. How many students from each grade level came along, and how many students were there?
64, 2

MADE AND DESIGNED 100% BY KIDS!

1. Nine of the students at Cinnamon Elementary School passed out a total of 1,917 flyers to the homes near school telling about the carnival on Saturday. How many flyers did each student pass out?
213

2. Frisbee' Elementary School printed its own student newspaper for the kids around town. A total of 2,910 copies were printed to distribute to 6 elementary schools. How many went to each school?
485

3. Barbara's school decided to give out the button that she designed to remind everyone to keep their city clean. The school printed a total of 1,729 buttons for both elementary schools in her town. How many did each school receive? How many extras were there?
864, 1

4. Monica was so excited when the local newspaper decided to print her comic strip in its evening edition! After the newspaper printed the first of her comic strips, it printed 2 more. All 3 editions came to a total of 1,958 copies. How many extras were printed in each edition? How many extras were printed at one of the editions?
652, 2

Division of Whole Numbers

5. A total of 1,670 tickets was printed for 7 performances of Rocky Road Elementary School's famous play, "Broccoli Pie!" How many tickets were printed for each performance? How many extras were printed?
238, 4

6. 4,635 students from 5 elementary schools each submitted a name that the new panda now living in the local city zoo should be called. How many different names did each school submit?
927

7. Mrs. Chimebell let her student Leon design the invitation for the school science fair. 1,408 invitations were printed and divided evenly among 8 grade levels. How many invitations were distributed to each grade level?
176

8. A total of 2,728 entries was received from 4 schools for the skateboard/rollerblade rodeo! How many entries were received from each school?
682

9. 1,924 students from 5 schools sent in a drawing of what they thought the new park downtown should look like. How many sketches came from each school? How many extras were received?
384, 4

10. The Parks and Recreation Department printed and distributed 5,568 flyers to 6 schools letting the kids around town know about the softball championship and celebration. How many flyers were sent to each school?
928

LET'S GO SEE "AMERICA THE BEAUTIFUL!"

1. A total of 483 students from Monica's school toured Crater Lake National Park. They took 6 buses. How many students were on each bus? How many extra students were on one of the buses?
80, 3

2. A total of 1,521 boys and girls from 3 schools enjoyed the magnificent caves at Carlsbad Caverns National Park! How many students came from each school?
507

3. There were 1,210 children from the 2 schools in Bill's town that visited Yosemite National Park in California. How many children from each school went?
605

4. Eight groups came out to see the glaciers at Glacier National Park in Montana. A total of 567 children enjoyed the trip. How many children were in each group? How many extras were there?
70, 7

5. During the school year, 9 schools visited Sequoia National Park in California! There were 1,872 students in all that got to see firsthand what a tree about 2,500 years old looks like and what it is like to drive right through the middle of a tree! How many students came from each school?
208

Division of Whole Numbers

5. 635 girls from Katelyn's scout troop wanted to hike down to see the Grand Canyon for themselves. They divided into 7 groups to make the trip. How many scouts were in each group? How many extras were there?
90, 5

7. 2,882 children from 3 towns made the trip to see Old Faithful in Yellowstone National Park last summer! How many children went from each town? How many extras were there?
960, 2

8. 202 boys and girls arrived on 5 buses to hike around and enjoy the Blue Ridge Mountains and the Shenandoah River in Shenandoah National Park. How many children came on each bus? How many were left over?
40, 2

9. Four groups of hikers wanted to North Cascades National Park to explore and have fun. A total of 240 boys and girls went. How many hikers were in each group that went to Washington?
60

10. A total of 1,202 students from 5 schools came to see and explore the animal fossils in Badlands National Park. How many students came from each school to visit this park in South Dakota? How many extra students came from one of the schools?
240, 2

11. Two groups of students flew to the island of Hawaii to see for themselves what an active volcano looks like! A total of 606 students made the exciting trip. How many students were in each group?
303

WE HAVE ENGINE IGNITION AND LIFT-OFF!

1. A total of 318 children was scheduled to go watch the space shuttle launch. Each bus was able to transport 53 children. How many buses were used?
6

2. 295 children's experiments were allowed on this shuttle's launch. They were placed in groups of 36. How many groups were there? How many children were left over to place separately?
8, 7

3. The amount of time the astronauts spent outside the shuttle repairing a satellite was 370 minutes. They went out each time for a period of 74 minutes. How many times did they go out?
5

4. A total of 186 engineers worked on the satellite that was being launched. 62 engineers worked on each section. How many sections were there to design and build?
3

5. There was a total of 264 heat shield tiles left to be placed on the new shuttle. 33 were put on each day. How many days did it take to finish this job?
8

Division of Whole Numbers

6. There was a total of 192 hours until lift-off of Discovery. How many days were left until the launch?
8

7. On one of the flights, a new course had to be made, and the engines burned for a total of 221 seconds. Each burning was a period of 65 seconds. How many times were the engines ignited? How many extra seconds did the engines burn on one of the ignitions?
3, 26

8. All 736 children sat around television monitors at Raleigh's school to watch the space shuttle Discovery launch into space! 92 children were huddled around each monitor. How many monitors did they have to view from?
8

9. There were 220 students in all that attended Space Camp during the summer! Each group had 41 boys and girls. How many groups met during the summer? How many extra students were in one?
5, 15

10. 174 people were seated in 87 cars along the road to watch the shuttle land. How many people were in each car?
2

11. A total of 90 students wanted to learn how to become astronauts. 21 students from each classroom wanted to send away for a list of training qualifications. How many classrooms were interested? How many extra students were in one of the classrooms?
4, 6

THERE'S LEARNING OUTSIDE THE CLASSROOM TOO!

1. This year, 903 children from 43 schools have visited the special space presentation at the planetarium. How many boys and girls were at each show?
21

2. Each day that the art museum was open, 75 children were allowed to spend time learning how to create sculptures with the artist. A total of 2,550 children spent time with the artist. How many days did the artist teach?
34

3. Already this year, 62,220 children have been able to enjoy the beautiful hay rides through the mountain preserve! There have been 34 trips by straw-filled wagons. How many children were on each wagon as it was pulled by horses? How many extra children were included?
18, 10

4. 51 groups have come to the library to hear the famous storyteller tell of old Indian legends. If there were 1,428 children in all, how many were in each group?
28

5. So far this year, 4,816 children have zoomed around the roller rink at the Roller Palace. 56 schools and groups have visited. How many children attended each visit?
86

Division of Whole Numbers

6. 1,549 students from 28 schools had visited George Washington's house and tomb in Mount Vernon, Virginia, when Eva's class arrived. How many students were from each school? How many extras were from one of the schools? **55, 9**

7. Last year, 91 classes visited Meteor Crater to see the gigantic hole left by the impact of the meteorite. A total of 3,276 children came in all. How many children come on each visit? **36**

8. 889 students from 22 schools have visited the Mineral Museum this year. How many students have attended from each school? How many extras have there been? **40, 9**

9. The local dairy has had 56 visits by schools in the area. A total of 4,622 students has come to learn about the production of milk and other dairy products. How many students have attended on each visit? How many extras have there been? **82, 30**

10. 861 students from 31 schools have come to see the ancient Indian ruins on the side of the mountain near town. How many students have attended on each visit? How many extras have attended? **27, 24**

11. In the first three months of this year, 1,262 students from 47 classrooms have visited Niagara Falls in New York! How many students have visited on each trip? How many extras have there been? **26, 40**

BUSINESS IS BOOMING TODAY!

1. When Merrill's Market advertised its 2-foot long cucumbers on sale, 8,733 of them were sold in 41 days. How many were sold each day? **213**

2. Buford's Burger Buffet sold 4,978 "big burgers" in 35 days. How many did it sell each day? How many extras did it sell? **142, 8**

3. Kathy's Clothing Closet could not believe the response from its newspaper and television ads. The store sold 15,210 pairs of its mouse shoes in 90 days. How many did it sell each day? **169**

4. Romelia's Roasted and Ready Restaurant sold 6,345 of its world famous boiled bags of peanuts in 15 days! How many bags did it sell each day? **423**

5. Mitchell's Microphone Mart sold 11,392 of its new slimline, wireless microphones in 64 days. The store found out that magazine advertising is just right for it. How many mikes did it sell each day? **178**

Division of Whole Numbers

6. Harry's Handyman Service received 9,792 calls in just 73 days. The phone was ringing off the wall! How many calls did it receive each day requesting work to be done? How many extra calls did it get? **134, 10**

7. Kelly's Corn Dog Stand sold 8,324 of its delectable dogs in the first 23 days of business. How many of these delicious dogs did the stand sell each day? How many extras did it sell? **361, 21**

8. Pete's Pipes and Sprinklers sold 8,500 pieces in just 32 days after putting up its new neon sign. How many pieces of pipe and such did it sell each day? How many extra pieces did it sell? **265, 20**

9. Stanley's Skateboard Stopover sold 5,838 really cool stickers that read, "I'm a Zoomer!" in just 14 days. The store couldn't believe the response! How many stickers did it sell each day? **417**

10. Felipe's Fence Factory just finished selling 7,987 fence posts in just 58 days! Certainly the beautiful fence that the company put around its store made a big difference! How many posts did it sell each day? How many extras did it sell? **137, 41**

11. David's Doorknob Directory helped 8,431 customers find the right doorknob for them in just 16 days. It was delightfully distracted by all the calls! How many customers did the service help each day? How many extras did it serve? **526, 15**

CLUBS ARE SO MUCH FUN!

1. All 7 members of the recyclable club found enough cans to earn $6.02 on their first trip cleaning up! How much money did each member earn? **$.86**

2. The 8 member rollerblade club happened upon an old purse with no identification. Inside was $13.76. How much did each member get if it was divided evenly? **$1.72**

3. While biking through the park, David and John kept cool by each bringing along a drink. They paid a total of $1.78 for these thirst quenchers. How much did each drink cost? **$.89**

4. All 39 members of the band received a ribbon to wear to show their school spirit during the faculty football game. The total cost was $32.76. How much did each ribbon cost? **$.84**

5. Mr. Kitklauder paid a total of $16.91 to buy all 19 members of the science club a special neon pencil that tells the temperature in Celsius degrees. How much did he pay for each pen? **$.89**

Division of Money

6. Theresa paid a total of $2.56 to buy 4 huge bones from the butcher to cook and give to her pooch to chew while she did her homework. What was the price of each bone? **$.64**

7. For the first hour of the car wash, 6 scrubbers and polishers of the student council brought in a total of $16.74 in donations for their school. How much does that equal in earnings for each worker? **$2.79**

8. All 16 members of the math club bought a baseball cap with the club's special logo on it. The members paid a total of $12.96. How much did each baseball cap cost? **$.81**

9. Nine students from Jolie's class ordered a special *What's Wrong With This Picture?* book. The order came to a total of $32.04. How much did each book cost? **$3.56**

10. Gabriel spent a total of $3.45 to buy herself and 4 other friends school spirit buttons. How much did she pay for each button? **$.69**

11. The fifth grade teachers bought a total of 56 treats for the students to enjoy during the special drama presentation. They paid a total of $37.52. What was the cost of each treat? **$.67**

12. Mrs. Moore ordered special pencils for her class that read, "You're Doing a Great Job!" She ordered 35 pencils for a total cost of $9.45. How much did she pay for each pencil? **$.27**

DECIMALS CAN BE SIMPLY DELIGHTFUL!

1. Jeff's mom was planning the most delicious salad that he would ever eat. She purchased 0.92 kg of snow peas, 1.3 kg of juicy, ripe tomatoes and 4.243 kg of jicama. How many kilograms of vegetables did she buy in all? **6.463**

2. Cyndi decided to build a birdhouse and other woodworking projects. She went to the store and bought 3.06 kg of long nails, 0.8 kg of finishing nails and 29.76 kg of all different types of wood. What was the total weight of her purchase? **33.62**

3. Michelle purchased 861.24 g of whole wheat flour and 289.19 g of cornmeal to make her famous corn muffins! How many grams of flour and cornmeal did she buy in all? **1150.43**

4. Al's science experiment called for 6.01 mL of vinegar and 3.14 mL of water. How many more milliliters of vinegar did he need? **2.87**

5. In one of the boxes of books in Kelly's room were 43.203 kg of comic books. That's a lot of comics! She took 12.419 kg of them so that she could try to lift the box. How much did the box of comics weigh after she took some out? **30.784**

Decimals

6. Eva put 6,214.3 L of water into her backyard pool. After splashing and jumping with her friends all day long, 1,821.9 L was knocked out. How many liters of water was left in the pool at the end of the day? **4392.4**

7. Each of the 5 sets of rollerblades weighed 8.93 kg. How much did they weigh in all? **44.65**

8. Four of the dogs that the students in Monica's class own weigh 41.2 kg each. How many kilograms is this? **164.8**

9. At David's school, an average of 1.29 days each year there are 18.3 children absent. How many absences is this in all? **23.607**

10. Both cages from the school science lab weighed 7.3 kg. How many kilograms did each of them weigh? **3.65**

11. As a math activity in Tom's class, the teacher asked him to weigh all 27 booklets. He found out that they weighed 16.2 kg altogether. What was the weight of each booklet? **.6**

12. Deborah found out that the pile of 42 paper clips she had weighed 26.46 g. What was the weight of each paper clip? **.63**

FRACTIONS DO ADD UP!

1. At Sonja's birthday party, 3/8 of her birthday cake was served to her friends. Another 1/8 was enjoyed by her family when she got home. What fraction of her cake was eaten? **4/8**

2. During Samuel's sleepover, 7/16 of the power in his batteries was used. Another 4/16 of the power was used when he practiced his new skit for the talent show. What fraction of the power was used? **11/16**

3. Virginia spent 1/7 of her allowance on fancy pencils for school. She spent another 4/7 of her allowance to go to the movies. What fraction of her allowance has she spent so far? **5/7**

4. During Kite Day at school, 3/10 of Richard's class wanted to fly box kites. Another 2/10 of his class wanted to fly regular trapezoid-shaped kites. What fraction of his class wanted to fly kites? **5/10**

5. In January, 3/9 of the animals at the Humane Society were cats. In February, 4/9 of the animals were little meowers! What was the total fraction of cats at the Humane Society during these two months? **7/9**

Addition of Fractions

6. During the first half of the soccer game, 7/15 of Andy's kicks were right on target. During the second half, another 7/15 of his kicks put the ball right where he wanted it. What fraction of his kicking was right on target during the game? **14/15**

7. Sophia nibbled on 4/11 of her apple during lunch. After school, she discovered that she had saved it in her lunch box and nibbled on another 3/11 of it! What fraction of her apple had Sophia eaten in all? **7/11**

8. In Vaughn's class, 4/10 of the students finished their state reports before they were due on Friday. An additional 3/10 of her class completed theirs on Friday. What fraction of the students in her class got the reports finished on time? **7/10**

9. At Anna's school, 8/20 of the students ordered fried chicken on Wednesday for lunch. Another 9/20 of the students ordered hamburgers. What fraction of the students ordered lunch? **17/20**

10. Rebecca gave her puppy 4/8 of the doggy biscuits in the box the first day she bought them. Boy, was her little tail wagger happy! During the rest of the week, she gave him another 3/8 of the biscuits. What fraction of the box has the cute, little puppy eaten so far? **7/8**

11. When Matthew arrived to have fun at the city pool, 2/5 of it was being used! While he was there, the pool filled up. What fraction of the pool was being used while Matthew was swimming? **3/5**

IT'S INCREDIBLY AMAZING THAT FRACTIONS CAN BE SUBTRACTED!

1. Ted's glass of cold, refreshing milk was $\frac{3}{4}$ full when he poured it. He drank $\frac{1}{4}$ of it just before his friend called on the phone. What fraction of it remained in the glass? **1/2**

2. At Purple Peach Elementary School, $\frac{9}{10}$ of the students rode their bikes to school. $\frac{1}{5}$ of them decided to take the new buses that were bought and stop riding their bikes. What fraction of the students still rode their bikes? **7/20**

3. Gerald invited $\frac{3}{4}$ of the boys in his class to his house to sleep over. Only $\frac{1}{2}$ were able to make it. What fraction of them couldn't come? **1/4**

4. Jim started out with $\frac{7}{8}$ of a bag of chips when he began his hike. He ate $\frac{1}{8}$ of the bag just going up the mountain! What fraction of the bag was left when he reached the top? **4/7**

5. At 9:00 a.m., $\frac{7}{9}$ of Connie's class had not seen the new baby rabbits in the science lab. At 9:05 a.m., $\frac{3}{9}$ went in to see them. What fraction of the class had still not seen them? **4/9**

Subtraction of Fractions

6. When Carl and his friends arrived home from school, $\frac{4}{5}$ of the watermelon was left in the refrigerator. They enjoyed $\frac{3}{5}$ of it while they sat around talking about the softball game at school. What fraction of the watermelon was left? **1/5**

7. Tiffany still needed to write $\frac{4}{5}$ of her thank you notes to all of her generous friends when she arrived home from school. Before she went to bed, she had written $\frac{3}{5}$ of them. What fraction of them did she still have to write? **1/5**

8. Shannon found out that $\frac{5}{9}$ of her friends had not finished their President reports on Friday. By Monday, $\frac{3}{9}$ had finished them. What fraction of her friends still needed to complete this assignment? **2/9**

9. On Saturday, $\frac{7}{10}$ of the popcorn seeds had not sprouted in Peter's planter. But by Sunday, $\frac{2}{10}$ of the little Indian corn had shot right out of the ground! What fraction of seeds now needed to germinate and break through the ground? **1/2**

10. When the kid in the paper came out, $\frac{5}{7}$ of the kittens were still at Barbara's house. At the end of the first day, $\frac{3}{7}$ of the remaining kittens had been given away to loving homes. What fraction of the kittens still remained? **1/4**

11. Melanie remembers when she was just a teensie weensie little girl in the first grade, she still had $\frac{7}{11}$ of her baby teeth! By second grade, she had lost another $\frac{5}{11}$ of them. What fraction of them did she need to lose after second grade? **2/11**

HOMEWORK; IT'S PART OF A KID'S LIFE!

1. Of the rocks that Marlene collected for science class, $\frac{7}{16}$ were igneous rock. Another $\frac{2}{16}$ were sedimentary rock. What fraction of the rocks that she collected are of these two types? **5/16**

2. Shasta drew $\frac{1}{6}$ of her cartoon character before art class. She sketched another $\frac{4}{6}$ of it during class. What fraction of her drawing did she finish? **5/6**

3. Joan completed $\frac{2}{7}$ of her math assignment during class. She also finished $\frac{1}{7}$ of her French lesson during study hall. What fraction of her homework did Joan finish at school? **3/7**

4. Last week, $\frac{1}{5}$ of David's music lesson was on sharps and flats, and $\frac{1}{5}$ of it was centered on practicing scales. What fraction of his lesson was focused on these two things? **2/5**

5. Clark read $\frac{3}{7}$ of his book about jets in the first sitting! He read another $\frac{2}{7}$ of it before school the next day! What fraction of his book has he read so far? **5/7**

Addition of Fractions

6. Archie used $\frac{1}{3}$ of his pencil writing a creative story about singing frogs! He used $\frac{1}{3}$ of his markers drawing the picture to go along with the story! What fraction of his pencil and markers did he use working on his funny story? **2/3**

7. In Alexa's book collection, $\frac{1}{6}$ are novels and $\frac{1}{5}$ are fact books about science. These two types are what fraction of her collection? **11/30**

8. John spent $\frac{3}{8}$ of his homework time working on his science project. Another $\frac{1}{4}$ of his time was spent practicing his trumpet! What fraction of his homework time was spent on these two activities? **5/8**

9. Daryl designed his sculpture using $\frac{1}{2}$ circles and $\frac{1}{3}$ trapezoid shapes. What fraction of his sculpture is made with these two shapes? **5/6**

10. Monica left $\frac{3}{6}$ of her garden empty to grow romaine lettuce in it. $\frac{1}{9}$ of her garden has juicy red tomatoes ready to be picked. What fraction of her garden is made up of these two vegetables? **7/18**

11. Rhonda chose to have $\frac{2}{5}$ of her report about France on the food that can be found there. She also decided to center another $\frac{1}{8}$ of it on words that we use in English that originated in France. What fraction of her report is focused on these two topics? **21/40**

AREN'T YOU GLAD THAT $\frac{3}{4}$ OF THE EARTH IS COVERED WITH WATER!

1. At the pond, $\frac{2}{7}$ of Bill's class met to ice-skate. $\frac{3}{14}$ had to leave after one hour of gliding and zooming around! What fraction of the class was left? **1/14**

2. At Travis' party, $\frac{3}{5}$ of the kids wanted to play basketball. $\frac{1}{10}$ decided to stop after they smelled the hamburgers on the grill. What fraction of the kids were still playing basketball? **1/2**

3. Of all Tim's friends, $\frac{5}{8}$ wanted to take the boat ride through the canyon. When they stopped to get off and climb around on the rocks, only $\frac{1}{4}$ of his friends wanted to do that. What fraction of his friends stayed on the boat? **3/8**

4. At the waterpark, $\frac{7}{10}$ of the children wanted to splash down the water slide! After a while, $\frac{3}{10}$ of them decided to get out and try surfing! What fraction of the children were still zooming down the water tunnels and splashing away? **2/5**

Subtraction of Fractions

5. At camp, $\frac{5}{9}$ of the kids wanted to try ice fishing. $\frac{3}{9}$ of them left after they tried it and decided to do something else. What fraction of the kids stayed and really loved it? **2/9**

6. At the end-of-the-year party, $\frac{3}{4}$ of the students wanted to have a squirt gun fight! $\frac{2}{4}$ of them surrendered after they realized how wet one can get in a challenge such as this! What fraction of the students continued playing? **1/4**

7. Of all the art students, $\frac{7}{15}$ wanted to learn how to make ice sculptures. $\frac{2}{15}$ of them changed their minds and wanted to work with ceramics. What fraction of the students decided to stay and learn about carving sculptures out of ice? **1/3**

8. At camp, $\frac{9}{14}$ of the kids said aloud "Yes!" to "Do you want to learn how to water-ski?" I had been given a turn by lunch time. What fraction of the kids still needed to try to learn? **5/14**

9. At the park, $\frac{9}{20}$ of the divers loved jumping off the high dive! $\frac{6}{20}$ of the divers wanted to try the low dive for a while. What fraction of the divers stayed on the high dive? **3/20**

10. In Cheri's class, $\frac{5}{12}$ of the students went on a trip to see the sea animal display in town. They loved watching the whales leap out of the water and glide through the air! $\frac{4}{12}$ of them wanted to rush right away and see the walruses do tricks too! What fraction of the students stayed to watch the whales? **1/12**

LET'S TRY SOME COORDINATE GEOMETRIC FRACTIONS!

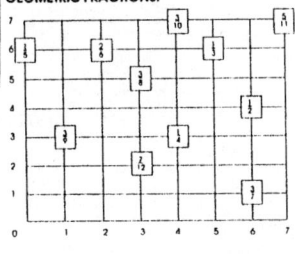

1. What is the sum of (0,6) and (4,7)? **1/2**
2. What is the difference of (3,2) and (6,4)? **1/12**
3. Which is greater: (3,2) or (2,6)? **(3,2)**
4. What is the coordinate for $\frac{1}{2}$? **(4,3)**
5. What is the sum of (7,7) and (5,6)? **26/33**

Using Coordinate Graphs

6. How much greater is (3,5) + (6,4) than (3,5) + (4,3)? **1/4**
7. What is the difference of (6,4) and (4,7)? **1/5**
8. What is the sum of (7,7) and (0,6)? **36/55**
9. What is the difference of (3,2) and (5,6)? **1/4**
10. Which is greater: (2,6) or (6,4)? **(6,4)**
11. How much greater is (6,1) than (5,6)? **2/21**
12. What is the sum of (4,3) and (2,6)? **7/12**

THERE'S MATH IN FOODS TOO!

1. At the musical performance of Bonnie's class, $9\frac{3}{6}$ of the apple pies and $7\frac{2}{6}$ of the cherry pies were eaten. How much of the pies had been eaten in all? **16 5/6**

2. At Shelly's class party, $2\frac{3}{10}$ of the cheese pizzas and $8\frac{2}{10}$ of the pepperoni pizzas were already gone! How much of the pizzas had been eaten so far? **10 7/10**

3. At the special dinner, $8\frac{1}{7}$ pieces of lasagna were served to the guests, and $5\frac{2}{7}$ were enjoyed by Maria's family the next night as leftovers! How much of the lasagna had been eaten in all? **13 3/7**

4. Carl was able to fit $6\frac{5}{8}$ of the birthday cakes on one platter, and $7\frac{3}{8}$ of the cakes on another platter! How much of the cakes did he get on both platters? **14 8**

5. Scott was very pleased to receive $5\frac{1}{8}$ pieces of asparagus on his plate! Esther was glad to get $3\frac{5}{8}$ pieces on her plate! How much asparagus did they receive in all? **9 6/8**

© 2006 Frank Schaffer Publications   E   0-88012-863-1

Addition of Mixed Numbers

6. Grant's doughnut statue was 1 5/8 meters high! Clayton's statue made of bakery delights was 1 6/8 meters high! How many meters high were both of them together? **3 3/8**

7. Debbie's pretzel was 3 2/3 inches long unrolled. Camille's pretzel was 6 1/3 inches in length unrolled. How long were the pretzels together? **9 4/9**

8. The letters of Roger's name were 8 1/2 cm tall. The letters of Gary's name were 8 1/2 cm tall. Both of them loved seeing their names on their birthday cakes! How many centimeters high were their names combined? **17**

9. It took Lydia 4 5/6 eggs to make her cake right. It took Candace 9 1/2 eggs to make her cake the way she wanted it. How many eggs did they use in all? **13 5/6**

10. Cyndi used 13 3/4 c of flour to make her special turkey pies! She also used 7 1/4 c of fresh carrots. How many cups of these two ingredients did she use? **21**

11. Forrest put in 12 1/3 L of root beer into the punch bowl. Then he added 9 1/3 L of vanilla ice cream! How many liters of ingredients did he use to make this fabulous drink? **21 2/3**

12. Brooke added 7 7/9 pt of strawberries to the ice cream mixture! Then she added 5 8/9 pt of bananas! How many pints of fruit did Brooke add to the homemade ice cream dessert? **13 5/9**

HOW LONG, HOW TALL, HOW FAR?

1. James could not believe how big Jack's tree fort was! It was 15 1/3 ft long and 6 1/3 ft wide! How many feet are these two dimensions when added together? **21 2/3**

2. Lonnie had to ride on the bus 4 1/8 miles to get to school. He also had to ride 9 3/8 miles to get to his piano teacher's house. What was the total distance he had to travel to get to these two places? **13 1/2**

3. Perry added 8 1/3 gal of water to his fish tank on the first bucket he put in. On the second bucket, he added another 7 2/3 gal. How much water did he put in his fish tank in all? **15 5/6**

4. This week, Kim fed her cats 13 3/4 c of cat food. Last week, she only fed them 6 1/4 c. How many cups of cat food in all did she feed her cute, little felines in the last two weeks? **19 23/30**

5. Peter rode his new scooter 5 1/4 times around the block today. Yesterday, he rode it 6 1/4 times around the block! How many times did he scoot around the block in all? **11 1/2**

Addition of Mixed Numbers

6. Charles measured his piece of beef jerky to be 9 1/4 in. long. Cliff measured his piece to be 9 1/3 in. length. How many inches were their pieces of beef jerky altogether? **18 7/12**

7. Eric's turtle weighed 9 3/8 lb, and his brother's turtle weighed 7 5/8 lb. How many pounds did the turtles weigh in all? **16 11/12**

8. The baby tegu lizards that Casey saw at the zoo were 12 1/2 in. long and 8 1/10 in. long. How long were they altogether? **20 7/15**

9. Hershel could not believe that it only took him 6 1/2 min to swim across the lake! His friend Graham could not believe that it only took him 7 3/10 min to cross the lake! How many minutes altogether did it take them to cross the lake? **13 7/10**

10. Sydel wove 2 3/4 ft of friendship rope last night while listening to her favorite music on the radio. Her friend Lynette was able to weave 5 1/4 ft of friendship rope when she got home from school. How many feet of rope did they weave in all? **8**

11. Christina's hair was 8 1/2 in. long after she got a haircut. She measured it 2 months later and found out that it grew another 1 1/7 in! How long is her hair now? **9 7/14**

12. Kelly could not believe how tall the stalks of corn in her garden were! One was 6 1/2 ft. tall, and the other was 7 1/4 ft tall. How high did the stalks reach for the sky in all? **13 3/4**

LET'S GET INTO SPORTS!

1. Stephanie was able to keep jogging for 9 1/8 miles before having to stop. She walked for the last 5/8 mile. How far did she go in all? **9 7/8**

2. Mark swam 8 1/2 laps doing the butterfly stroke! For 5/8 of a lap, he just swam freestyle. How far in all did he swim? **9 1/4**

3. Karen filled up the cooler with 15 1/4 gal of ice cold water. She added another 1/4 gal to fill it to the top. How many gallons of water are in the cooler now? **15 1/2**

4. Melissa rode her bike for 3 1/10 miles to get to her friend's house. After they got together, they rode another 3/10 of a mile to go to their favorite movie theater! How far did Melissa ride in all to get to the movie theater? **4 1/10**

5. Cyndi climbed 6 7/8 feet of the rope before having to stop. After taking a few breaths, she climbed another 3/10 of a foot. How far did she climb up the rope in all? **7 1/10**

Addition of Mixed Numbers

6. Viola could not believe that she could jump 5 1/10 ft into the air on the trampoline. On her next try, she added another 3/5 of a foot! How far did she jump on the second try? **6 3/10**

7. Laurie walked 7 2/3 miles for the walkathon when she thought she would drop right in her tracks! After a brief rest, she got up and walked another 1/3 mile. How far did she walk in all? **8**

8. Grant was able to swim under water for 3 1/3 laps without coming up for a breath! His friends were impressed. The next time, he went another 2/3 of a lap farther! How far did he go under water on the second try? **4 1/7**

9. Tricia lifted 5 1/4 lb of heavy weights over her head! She stopped and added another 1/4 of a pound. How many pounds of weights could she lift over her head now? **5 5/8**

10. Dale jumped 5 1/3 ft on his first try at the running long jump. On his second try, he jumped another 1/3 of a foot. How many feet did he jump on the second try? **6 1/12**

11. Trevor, after much practice, was able to clear 4 1/3 ft on the high jump! But, he didn't want to stop just yet! He had the coach add another 2/3 of a foot to the height of the pole. How many feet would he have to clear now? **4 5/6**

12. Duane was able to run to the store and back in 14 2/7 min. He tried running again without a rest and only added another 3/7 of a minute onto his time. How fast did he run to the store and back the second time? **14 5/7**

AREN'T REPTILES JUST THE CUTEST THINGS?

1. Mattie's gecko measured 11 1/2 in. long. Her brother's gecko measured 9 1/2 in. long. How much longer was Mattie's gecko? I wonder whose barked the loudest! **2 1/2**

2. Lynn's race runner lizard was 6 3/4 in. long. Her baby green lizard was 3 1/4 in. long. How much longer was her race runner lizard? **3 1/4**

3. Sandy's skink was 10 1/2 in. long. Her sandfish was 7 1/3 in. long. How much longer was her skink? **3 4/5**

4. Sean's flap-necked chameleon was 12 1/2 in. long. His body alone was 6 1/4 in. long. How long was his tail? **6 1/2**

5. Westie's pet soa-soa water dragon looked just like a dinosaur! It was 17 1/4 in. long. I guess he was a little small for a dinosaur, don't you think? His tail alone was 9 1/4 in. long. How long was his body? **8 1/3**

Subtraction of Mixed Numbers

6. Martha's baby basilisk lizard was the greenest lizard any of her friends had ever seen! It was 11 1/3 in. long, but she knew that it would soon grow to be 31 1/3 in. long! How many inches did it have to grow? **20 2/3**

7. Sarah's pretty blue collared lizard was a total of 9 1/5 in. long. Her Texas horned lizard was 7 1/5 in. long. How much longer was her collared lizard? **2 4/5**

8. Eric's spiny, soft shelled turtle was 15 1/2 in. long. His young matamata was 9 1/2 in. long. What an incredible turtle! How much longer was his spiny, soft-shelled turtle? **6 4/7**

9. Allen had two murray river turtles. One was 11 1/2 in. long, and the other was 8 1/6 in. long. What is the difference in their lengths? **3 1/3**

10. Alex's alligator snapping turtle was only 7 1/4 in. long. It had a ways to go before it was full grown. It was only 5 1/4 in. long when he first got it. How many inches had it grown since he first brought it home? **2 4/5**

11. Darren's gopher tortoise was 13 1/3 in. long. His wood turtle was 8 1/3 in. length. How much longer was his gopher tortoise? **5 3/9**

12. Andy's slowworm was 14 1/3 in. long. His California legless lizard was only 6 1/8 in. long. How much longer was his slowworm? **8 3/8**

HEAD 'EM UP, IT'S TIME TO HIKE!

1. Holly's granola bar weighs 3 3/4 oz. and her gum weighs 1 1/10 oz. How many more ounces does her granola bar weigh? **2 1/2**

2. Gary's canteen weighs 7 2/3 lb. and his binoculars weigh 3 1/3 lb. How much more does his canteen weigh? **4**

3. Glenn and his classmates were going to hike the full 6 1/2 miles through the forest. But they had to stop 2 1/3 miles short and turn around. How far did they hike into the forest? **4 4/9**

4. David and his friends took 14 4/10 gal of water on their hike. They drank 8 1/4 gal of water in the first few hours. How many gallons of water did they have left? **6 1/10**

5. Brigitte's backpack weighed 16 3/4 lb when she started her hike. After two days, she lost 9 1/4 lb by using up the goodies inside! How many pounds does her backpack weigh now? **7 1/10**

Subtraction of Mixed Numbers

6. Claire and her classmates had planned to hike a total of 12 10/10 miles in the week that they were camping. Due to lots of sore feet, they decided to limit it to 7 2/10 miles. How many miles did they shave off their trip? **5 3/10**

7. Daniel started out with 13 5/8 lb in his backpack. After careful pondering and decisive moves to lighten it, he eliminated 7 1/4 lb! How many pounds did his backpack weigh after he got rid of some of the weight? **6 1/3**

8. Earl's fishing group caught a total of 14 1/3 lb of fish. The group cooked up 9 1/3 lb the first day but then kept the rest. How many pounds of fish were left to enjoy? **5**

9. Altogether Paul's class found and kept 18 3/4 lb of rocks. The students decided the rocks were getting too heavy, so they put back 9 1/4 lb. How many pounds did they end up keeping? **9 5/7**

10. Gary picked 9 3/8 lb of fruit on this hike! But he ate 5 1/2 lb coming back! How much fruit did he have left when he got back? **4 3/8**

11. Charlie could not believe that his backpack accumulated an extra 6 1/8 lb after getting wet in the rain! After it dried in the sun, it lost 3 2/21 lb. How many pounds did the backpack have to lose to return to its original weight? **3 13/21**

HOW FAR IS IT GOING TO BE?

Using a Map

5. How many kilometers is it from Tunnel Mountain to Splasher Lake passing over Chris-Cross Bridge? **21 3/4**

6. How much farther is it to travel from Chris-Cross Bridge to Tunnel Mountain than it is to travel from Chris-Cross Bridge to Splasher Lake? **5 1/3**

7. How far is the shortest route from Chris-Cross Bridge to Boulder Park? **14 1/2**

8. What is the difference to travel from Chris-Cross Bridge to Tunnel Mountain as compared to travelling from Boulder Park to Cat City? **6 1/6**

9. Which is the shortest route from Tunnel Mountain to Splasher Lake? **C+C+BP**

10. Which route starting at Boulder Park is a distance of 13 kilometers? **Tm-C**

11. Which is the shortest route from Cat City to Chris-Cross Bridge? **BP+SL**

12. Here's a real challenge to prove how smart you are! Can you figure out how far you would travel if you started at Tunnel Mountain, crossed through all the landmarks and ended up back at Tunnel Mountain? **40 7/9**

1. How much farther is it from Chris-Cross Bridge to Splasher Lake than from Boulder Lake to Boulder Park? **15/6**

2. How many kilometers is it to travel from Tunnel Mountain to Boulder Park, passing through Cat City? **12 7/9**

3. How far is it to travel from Chris-Cross Bridge to Cat City passing through Tunnel Mountain? **20 5/6**

4. How far is it to travel from Splasher Lake to Cat City passing through Boulder Park? **11 7/9**

ART IS SUCH A GREAT WAY TO EXPRESS YOURSELF!

1. Wendy was helping to draw a title for the yearbook page that her class was designing. It started out 5 7/8 inches long. She shortened it by 3/8 of an inch. How long is it now? **5 4/7**

2. Rochelle added 3 1/8 cups of flour to her famous cookie recipe. Realizing she had a tad too much, she scooped out 1/4 of a cup. How many cups of flour did she end up putting in her cookie batter? **3 3/8**

3. Kevin's ceramic bowl was 6 7/8 inches in diameter. After looking it over, he decided to narrow it by 1/8 of an inch. What is the diameter of his bowl now? **6 4/5**

4. Pam's drawing was 9 7/8 inches wide. But, in order to make it fit nicely into the picture frame, she had to trim off 1/3 of an inch. What is the width of her drawing now? **9 8/21**

5. Suzanne's bean mosaic was only 2 5/8 inches wide. She decided to trim off 1/8 of an inch on one side. How wide is this miniature mosaic now? **2 4/5**

Subtraction of Mixed Numbers

6. Gabriel poured 7 3/8 cups of water into his mixture of plaster of Paris. When he saw that it was just a little too much, he drained off 1/3 of a cup. How much water did he end up adding? **7 1/6**

7. Sophia had woven a colorful friendship bracelet that was 10 1/4 inches long. She felt that it was just a tiny bit too long and trimmed off 1/8 of an inch. How long is her bracelet now? **10 1/2**

8. Carmen's papier-mâché planet started out being 5 3/8 inches in diameter. After it dried, it shrunk 1/10 of an inch. What was the diameter of his planet after it dried? **5 3/10**

9. Cheryl placed 2 7/8 oz of colored ink on the plate for her spin art project. Just before she started it up, she took off 1/3 of an ounce, thinking that it was too much! How many ounces of ink did she end up using? **2 1/3**

10. Joni carefully placed 4 1/8 lb of clay on her potter's wheel. She immediately carved off 1/4 of a pound and placed it on the table by her side. How much clay did she have on her wheel? **4 1/8**

11. Tiffany started out with 3 2/3 oz of miniature beads to make her bracelet. She saw that her friend didn't quite have enough and immediately gave her 1/2 of an ounce of beads. How many ounces of beads did she end up using? **3**

12. Bill's family animal collage was originally 8 7/8 in. wide. He trimmed off 1/4 of an inch from one side to even it out! How wide is it now? **8 5/8**

CAN YOU REALLY TAKE A "PART" OF SOMETHING FROM A "WHOLE" OF SOMETHING?

1. Lionel squeezed 6 cups of fresh orange juice to share with his family! He scooped out 3/8 of a cup of seeds. How many cups of juice did he end up with? **5 5/8**

2. Murray tried to fill 12 oz of ice water into his canteen. He had to pour out 1/2 of an ounce to get the lid on without spilling the water. How much water was he able to fit in his canteen? **11 1/2**

3. Lowell had 3 lb of pomegranates to share with his friends as an after-school snack. Lowell enjoyed 3/4 of a pound and gave the rest to his friends. How many pounds of this delicious fruit did he give to his friends to enjoy? **2 1/2**

4. Stacy put 8 oz of cat food in her kitty's dish. When the cat was finished eating, there was 2/3 of an ounce of food left in the dish. How many ounces did Stacy's cat eat in all? **7 8/11**

5. Royal bought 5 lb of black seedless grapes to have in his lunches. He took 4/7 of a pound with him the first day. How many pounds did he have left for the rest of the week? **4 4/7**

Subtraction of Fractions

6. Tracy started to drink her 12 oz glass of milk when she happened to glance down and see her cute, little snowball kitten peeking up at her. She poured 3/8 of an ounce of milk in a little bowl for her kitten. How many ounces of milk did she end up drinking herself? **11 2/9**

7. Tricia picked 7 baskets of apricots while visiting her cousin's farm. Since some of the apricots were overripe, 2/3 of a basket had to be thrown away. How many baskets did Tricia take home with her? **6 3/5**

8. Adam bought 14 lb of dog food for his faithful, little tailwagger! He poured 2/3 of a pound into the doggie bowl as soon as he arrived home. How many pounds were left in the bag? **13 3/4**

9. Linda made a 9 oz banana-milk drink in the blender. Bananas made up 2/3 of an ounce of the drink. How many ounces of the drink was made with milk? **8 2/3**

10. Mark picked up 15 cans of tuna fish while shopping with his mom at the grocery store. As soon as he got home, he made a tuna fish sandwich and used 3/5 of a can on his bread. How many cans of tuna fish were left? **14 4/5**

11. Pamela's family purchased 3/5 of a pound short of 20 lb of watermelon for its family picnic on Saturday. How many pounds of watermelon were bought? **19 4/5**

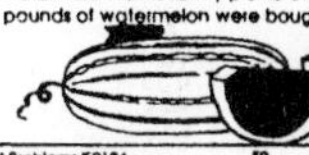

IF YOU'VE GOT A CHOICE, PICK SCIENCE!

1. In David's class, 2/3 of the boys built model rockets to launch. Streamers were used on 1/5 of the rockets to slow them down instead of parachutes. What fraction of the boys built rockets that had streamers? **2/15**

2. In Heather's class, 1/4 of the students wanted to help build the huge papier-mâché volcano. Of the students that helped, 3/7 got covered in papier-mâché mess. What fraction of the students got all messy? **3/28**

3. On Saturday, 3/7 of Debbie's class volunteered to help clean the park grounds to help get them ready for the big science show! Can you believe that 7/9 of the class stayed all day to help! What fraction of the class was able to stay all day? **3/11**

4. A total of 5/8 of the boys in Mark's scout troop built and designed their own skateboards. 3/5 of these skateboards were built with oak. What fraction of the scouts made skateboards using oak? **3/8**

Multiplication of Fractions

5. At Clifford's school, 2/3 of the students wanted to learn about the new science museum that was just built. This month, 1/5 of the students were able to go see it. What fraction of students were able to go see it right away? **1/15**

6. Lots of people came to watch the space shuttle land. Of these people, 7/8 were students from California and 3/8 of the students were fifth graders! What fraction of these students were fifth graders? **3/14**

7. Making fossils out of plaster of Paris is fun. That's why 1/10 of Matthew's class chose to make them. Only 2/3 of these students used shells to make their imprints in their plaster. What fraction of the class used shells? **1/4**

8. On Saturday, 2/3 of Peter's class came to school to learn how to make solar ovens. Pizzas were cooked by 3/8 of the students who came. What fraction of the class chose to cook pizza? **1/4**

9. Cecilia used 2/3 of her balloons to learn about static electricity by rubbing them on her head and sticking them to things. After lunch, 3/7 of the balloons were still sticking to the wall! What fraction were still sticking to the wall? **9/28**

10. For the hot air balloon demonstrations and rides on Saturday, 5/9 of Curt's class attended. Can you believe that 7/8 of the students were brave enough to want to ride in the balloons? What fraction of the class wanted to take a ride? **30/49**

IT'S TIME TO PACK YOUR TENT!

1. Out of Diana's classmates, 5/8 wanted fresh maple syrup poured on their homemade ice cream! There were 32 students in her class. How many wanted syrup on their ice cream? **20**

2. On Wednesday morning, 2/3 of Mike's classmates put blueberries on their cereal! If there are 27 students in Mike's class, how many put blueberries on their cereal? **18**

3. After lunch, 2/3 of Jeff's class wanted to go fishing. Jeff had 24 students in his classroom. How many wanted to go fishing? **12**

4. There were 36 girls that attended Cheryl's scouting trip. Of the girls, 1/2 of them wanted to go hunting for wild strawberries! How many went on the search? **18**

5. Of the 49 kids on the campout, 2/7 wanted to go to bed right after the sing-along around the fire. How many kids wanted to hit the sack right away? **14**

© 2006 Frank Schaffer Publications   G   0-88012-863-1

Multiplication of Fractions

6. Out of the 18 campers, $\frac{1}{9}$ used water to make soup their first night out. How many campers made soup with water?

2

7. Making biscuits over the open fire looked like so much fun that $\frac{5}{6}$ of the 24 campers wanted to learn how. How many campers learned how to make biscuits?

20

8. Since the water in the campers' canteens was not very cold, $\frac{7}{8}$ of the campers wanted ice. If there were 16 campers, how many wanted ice for their canteens?

14

9. Of the 25 students in Whitney's class, $\frac{3}{5}$ wanted to have fresh blackberries on top of their cereal. How fortunate they were to find the wild berries near their campsite! How many students wanted these wild berries?

15

10. 48 students from Andy's class went on the overnight. When it was time to hunt for geodes, $\frac{2}{8}$ of the students wanted to stay behind. How many students wanted to stay behind in all?

12

11. A total of 36 campers attended the trip to the lake. The water looked so inviting that $\frac{2}{12}$ of the campers wanted to go swimming right away! How many wanted to get in the water as soon as possible?

6

12. The hike to the canyon looked so difficult that only $\frac{5}{11}$ of the 44 campers from Donna's scouting group went. How many hiked to the canyon in all?

20

MULTIPLYING MIXED NUMBERS WILL NOT MIX YOU UP!

1. John filled $1\frac{1}{4}$ buckets full of interesting rocks from his hike. Of these rocks, $\frac{3}{5}$ of them were rose quartz. How much of the bucket was filled with rose quartz?

3/4

2. Ronald found $2\frac{1}{5}$ cups of acorns on the ground. Of these acorns, $\frac{2}{7}$ of them were dried out and ready for planting. How many cups of acorns were ready for planting?

22/35

3. Joan put $2\frac{2}{8}$ cups of sand in the bottom of her aquarium. A lot of the sand was dark brown, but $\frac{2}{9}$ of it was white. How many cups were white sand?

1/2

4. Marlene put $2\frac{1}{2}$ cups of food in her dog's bowl for dinner. Fresh gravy made up $\frac{2}{5}$ of the food. How much of her dog's dinner was gravy?

1

5. Leo used $3\frac{1}{2}$ inches of ribbon to wrap his special birthday present. Only $\frac{3}{8}$ of the ribbon was used to make the bow. How much ribbon was used to make the bow?

15/16

Multiplication of Mixed Numbers

6. Kimiko put $1\frac{1}{9}$ cups of salt into the jar full of water to make salt crystals. Only $\frac{1}{8}$ of the salt would not mix with the water solution. How much of the salt did not mix with the water after the solution became saturated?

5/36

7. Kay bought $2\frac{1}{6}$ lb of grapes at the store. She put $\frac{3}{5}$ of them out in the sun on a special tray to make her own raisins! How many pounds of raisins did she make?

1 3/10

8. Daniel put $2\frac{2}{3}$ gal of water into his fish tank. Then he decided to remove $\frac{1}{3}$ of the water. How many gallons of water did he remove?

8/9

9. Janet put $2\frac{1}{5}$ oz of peanut butter into her cookie mix. She scooped out $\frac{3}{7}$ of it when she realized that it looked like too much. How many ounces of peanut butter did she scoop out?

33/35

10. Julius filled up his piggy bank with $1\frac{2}{9}$ cups of coins. If $\frac{3}{5}$ of the coins were dimes, how much of the bank was filled with dimes?

11/15

11. There were $2\frac{1}{6}$ gal of water left in the water cooler when Dixie woke up. After her dad and brother finished mowing the yard, they drank $\frac{3}{8}$ of the water. How many gallons of water did they drink?

13/16

LET'S MEASURE IT AND THEN MAKE IT!

1. Francisco cut 5 pieces of wood into $1\frac{2}{3}$ ft lengths each. How many feet does this equal in all?

8 1/3

2. Todd used two $1\frac{1}{4}$ ft long pieces of plastic to make his colorful book cover. How many feet was the plastic in all?

2 1/2

3. Gary used 3 pieces of nylon string to weave his rope. Each piece was $3\frac{1}{4}$ feet long. How long were the strings altogether?

9 3/4

4. Nine students in Alex's class each used a piece of balsa wood $2\frac{1}{6}$ ft long to make their airplanes. How many feet of balsa wood did the class use in all?

19 1/2

5. Each of Carolyn's 2 pieces of leather were $3\frac{1}{6}$ inches long. How long were they altogether?

6 1/3

Multiplication of Fractions

6. Each of the 4 branches that Cheryl was going to use for the macramé was $5\frac{1}{2}$ feet long. How long were they in all?

22

7. Each of the 7 pieces of plywood that Bill was going to use for his tree fort were $1\frac{1}{5}$ feet long. How long were the pieces of wood altogether?

8 2/5

8. Both of the rocks that Sarah was going to use to make her necklace were $1\frac{1}{3}$ inches long. How long were they in all?

2 2/3

9. Each of the 8 pieces of felt that Shelly was using to decorate her puppets with was $2\frac{1}{7}$ inches wide. How wide in all was the felt that she was using?

17 1/7

10. Five times Christina added $1\frac{1}{9}$ cups of flour to make her pizza dough. How much dough did she use in all?

5 5/9

11. Each of the 3 designs that Steven cut out was $2\frac{1}{5}$ feet in diameter. How many feet in diameter were they altogether?

6 3/5

12. Michelle used 6 bolts that were each $1\frac{2}{7}$ inches long to fasten her wood project together. What was the total length of the bolts?

7 5/7

FOOD AND DIVISION WERE MEANT FOR EACH OTHER!

1. Eva's classmates bought 5 pizzas to help celebrate all their successes in math. Each student received a slice that was $\frac{1}{8}$ of a pizza. How many slices did they cut up?

40

2. Eleven cantaloupes were brought to serve for the class breakfast. Each student received $\frac{1}{4}$ of a cantaloupe. How many pieces were served in all?

44

3. There were 6 pies at the carnival for the pie-eating contest. Each contestant received a slice that was $\frac{1}{9}$ of a pie. How many slices were cut to use for this event?

54

4. There was a total of 2 pounds of apples to make the apple treats. Each treat contained $\frac{1}{5}$ of a pound of apples. How many treats were made?

10

5. Five blocks of ice were used to make the snow cones. Each snow cone used $\frac{1}{8}$ of a block. How many snow cones were made from these blocks of ice?

40

Division of Fractions

6. Richard's dad bought 7 bottles of mineral water to drink at the park. Each cup that he drank held $\frac{1}{7}$ of a bottle. How many cups was he able to drink?

49

7. There were 3 small cakes at Roger's birthday party. Each child received a piece that was $\frac{2}{6}$ of one cake. How many children attended Roger's birthday party in all?

9

8. Eight watermelons were brought to the family picnic and sliced. Each slice was $\frac{1}{7}$ of a watermelon. How many slices were served?

56

9. Earl's mom and dad bought 4 submarine sandwiches and divided them into pieces. Each piece was $\frac{1}{6}$ of a sandwich. How many pieces did they make after cutting up the sandwiches?

24

10. Six stalks of celery were used to make the "bumps on a log" treats. Each treat was made with $\frac{1}{3}$ of a stalk of celery. How many treats were made in all?

18

11. Two bottles of ketchup were brought to put on the hamburgers at Samuel's party. On each child's burger, $\frac{1}{7}$ of a bottle was used. How many burgers were served at his party?

14

12. Four containers of milk were brought to serve cereal with. Each student had $\frac{1}{5}$ of a container poured on top of his/her cereal. How many students did this milk serve?

20

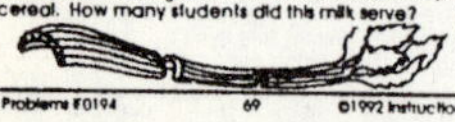

HERE'S A CHANCE TO PROVE YOURSELF!

1. Holly's Market ordered 54,123 lb of food 32 times this year. How many pounds of food did the market order in all this year?

1,731,936

2. Julio bought 5 bags of vegetables that each weighed $3\frac{1}{2}$ pounds. How many pounds did his purchase weigh in all?

17 1/2

3. Bruce paid a total of $50.80 for 8 model rocket kits. He bought them for himself and his other friends in his scout troop. How much did he pay for each rocket kit?

$6.35

4. Four schools brought a total of 2,276 champion math students to the national conference on how kids can make math more fun! How many students attended from each school?

569

5. At the pound, $\frac{3}{7}$ of the dogs were poodles. Of the poodles, $\frac{2}{5}$ were white and fluffy. What fraction of the dogs were fluffy white poodles?

6/35

Choosing the Operation

6. Monica arrives for school at 8:15 a.m. She spends all day at school except for the 1 hour and 15 minutes that she leaves campus to attend her drama class. She leaves school at 4:30 p.m. How many hours does Monica spend at school in all?

7

7. An average of 6.8 of the rainy days in Purple Frog had 3.91 inches of rain. How much rain is this in all?

26.588

8. Jennifer picked $\frac{2}{7}$ of an ounce of flowers from her garden on Tuesday. On Wednesday, she picked another $\frac{3}{21}$ of an ounce. How many ounces in all did she pick?

3/7

9. Eight bags of fresh roasted peanuts were purchased for the kids watching the over-sized trucks trying to climb the mud hills! Each child was given $\frac{1}{3}$ of a bag of peanuts. How many children did these bags of peanuts serve?

24

10. Russell bought $9\frac{2}{5}$ lb of food for his tegu lizard, his loco toucan and his pretty, little kitty cat. He also bought $3\frac{4}{5}$ lb of vegetables and fruit for himself. How many pounds of food did he buy in all?

13 1/5

11. The circulation of the *Podunk Times* is 382,194 copies per edition. The closest newspaper is the *Green Leaf Gazette*, which has a circulation of 96,215 newspapers per edition. How many more newspapers does the *Podunk Times* print for each edition?

285,979

0-88012-863-1

Subtraction of Fractions

6. When Carl and his friends arrived home from school, $\frac{8}{15}$ of the watermelon was left in the refrigerator. They enjoyed $\frac{5}{15}$ of it while they sat around talking about the softball game at school. What fraction of the watermelon was left?

7. Tiffany still needed to write $\frac{4}{5}$ of her thank-you notes to all of her generous friends when she arrived home from school. Before she went to bed, she had written $\frac{3}{5}$ of them. What fraction of them did she still have to write?

8. Shannon found out that $\frac{8}{9}$ of her friends had not finished their President reports on Friday. By Monday, $\frac{6}{9}$ had finished them. What fraction of her friends still needed to complete this assignment?

9. On Saturday, $\frac{9}{10}$ of the popcorn seeds had not sprouted in Peter's planter. But by Sunday, $\frac{4}{10}$ of the little Indian corn had shot right out of the ground! What fraction of seeds still needed to germinate and break through the ground?

10. When the ad in the paper came out, $\frac{9}{12}$ of the kittens were still at Barbara's house. At the end of the first day, $\frac{6}{12}$ of the remaining kittens had been given away to loving homes. What fraction of the kittens still remained?

11. Melanie remembers when she was just a teensie weensie little girl in the first grade, and she still had $\frac{6}{11}$ of her baby teeth! By second grade, she had lost another $\frac{4}{11}$ of them. What fraction of them did she need to lose after second grade?

HOMEWORK; IT'S PART OF A KID'S LIFE!

1. Of the rocks that Marlene collected for science class, $\frac{1}{8}$ were igneous rock. Another $\frac{3}{16}$ were sedimentary rock. What fraction of the rocks that she collected are of these two types?

2. Shasta drew $\frac{1}{3}$ of her cartoon character before art class. She sketched another $\frac{1}{2}$ of it during class. What fraction of her drawing did she finish?

3. Joan completed $\frac{2}{7}$ of her math assignment during class. She also finished $\frac{3}{21}$ of her French lesson during study hall. What fraction of her homework did Joan finish at school?

4. Last week, $\frac{1}{5}$ of David's music lesson was on sharps and flats, and $\frac{2}{10}$ of it was centered on practicing scales. What fraction of his lesson was focused on these two things?

5. Clark read $\frac{1}{2}$ of his book about jets in the first sitting! He read another $\frac{3}{14}$ of it before school the next day! What fraction of his book has he read so far?

Addition of Fractions

6. Archie used $\frac{2}{4}$ of his pencil writing a creative story about singing frogs! He used $\frac{2}{12}$ of his markers drawing the picture to go along with the story! What fraction of his pencil and markers did he use working on his funny story?

7. In Alexa's book collection, $\frac{1}{5}$ are novels and $\frac{1}{6}$ are fact books about science. These two types are what fraction of her collection?

8. John spent $\frac{3}{8}$ of his homework time working on his science project. Another $\frac{1}{4}$ of his time was spent practicing his trumpet! What fraction of his homework time was spent on these two activities?

9. Daryl designed his sculpture using $\frac{1}{2}$ circles and $\frac{2}{6}$ trapezoid shapes. What fraction of his sculpture is made with these two shapes?

10. Monica left $\frac{2}{9}$ of her garden empty to grow romaine lettuce in it. $\frac{3}{18}$ of her garden has juicy red tomatoes ready to be picked! What fraction of her garden is made up of these two vegetables?

11. Rhonda chose to have $\frac{2}{5}$ of her report about France on the food that can be found there. She also decided to center another $\frac{1}{8}$ of it on words that we use in English that originated in France. What fraction of her report is focused on these two topics?

AREN'T YOU GLAD THAT $\frac{3}{4}$ OF THE EARTH IS COVERED WITH WATER!

1. At the pond, $\frac{2}{7}$ of Bill's class met to ice-skate. $\frac{3}{14}$ had to leave after one hour of gliding and zooming around! What fraction of the class was left?

2. At Travis' party, $\frac{3}{5}$ of the kids wanted to play basketball. $\frac{1}{10}$ decided to stop after they smelled the hamburgers on the grill! What fraction of the kids were still playing basketball?

3. Of all Tim's friends, $\frac{5}{8}$ wanted to take the boat ride through the canyon. When they stopped to get off and climb around on the rocks, only $\frac{1}{4}$ of his friends wanted to do that. What fraction of his friends stayed on the boat?

4. At the waterpark, $\frac{8}{10}$ of the children wanted to splash down the water slide! After a while, $\frac{2}{5}$ of them decided to get out to try surfing! What fraction of the children were still zooming down the water tunnels and splashing away?

© 2006 Frank Schaffer Publications

Subtraction of Fractions

5. At camp, $\frac{5}{9}$ of the kids wanted to try ice fishing. $\frac{1}{3}$ of them left after they tried it and decided to do something else. What fraction of the kids stayed and really loved it?

6. At the end-of-the-year party, $\frac{1}{2}$ of the students wanted to have a squirt gun fight! $\frac{2}{8}$ of them surrendered after they realized how wet one can get in a challenge such as this! What fraction of the students continued playing?

7. Of all the art students, $\frac{9}{15}$ wanted to learn how to make ice sculptures. $\frac{2}{5}$ of them changed their minds and wanted to work with ceramics. What fraction of the students decided to stay and learn about carving sculptures out of ice?

8. At camp, $\frac{6}{7}$ of the kids said a loud "Yes!" to "Do you want to learn how to water-ski?" $\frac{1}{2}$ had been given a turn by lunch time. What fraction of the kids still needed to try to learn?

9. At the park, $\frac{5}{20}$ of the divers loved jumping off the high dive! $\frac{1}{10}$ of the divers wanted to try the low dive for awhile. What fraction of the divers stayed on the high dive?

10. In Cheri's class, $\frac{5}{12}$ of the students went on a trip to see the sea animal display in town. They loved watching the whales leap out of the water and glide through the air! $\frac{2}{6}$ of them wanted to rush right away and see the walruses do tricks too! What fraction of the students stayed to watch the whales?

LET'S TRY SOME COORDINATE GEOMETRIC FRACTIONS!

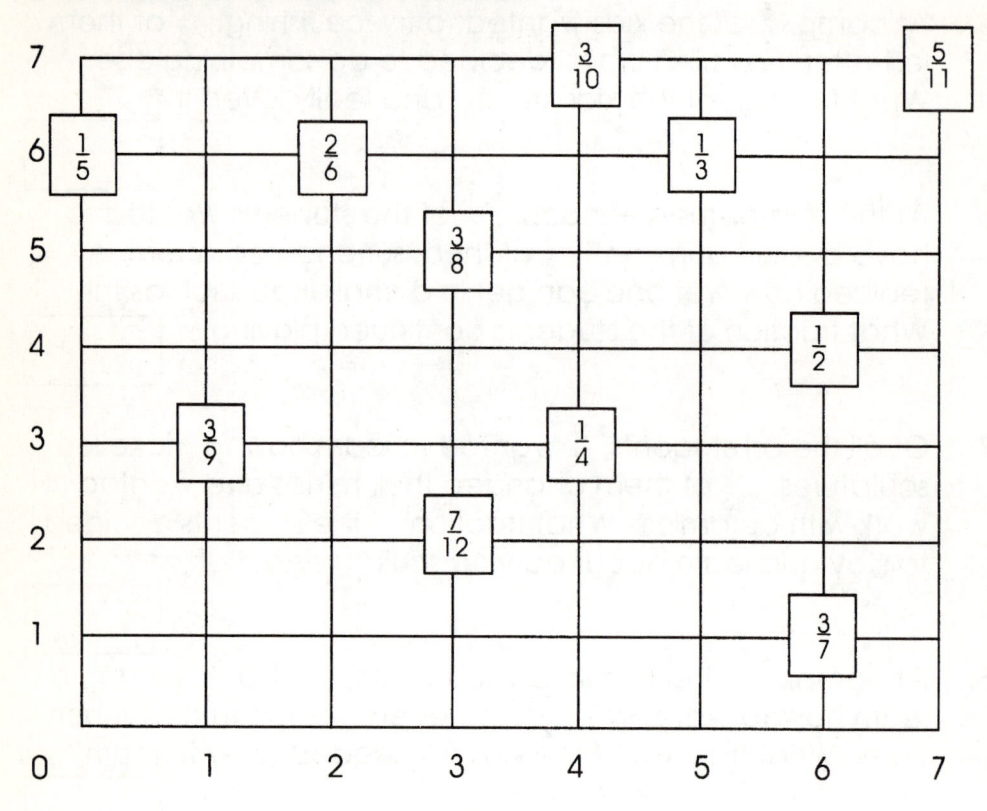

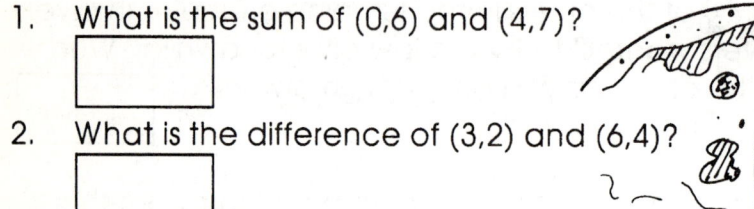

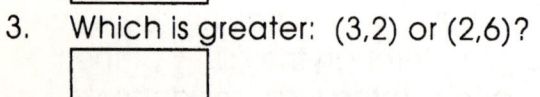

7				$\frac{3}{10}$			$\frac{5}{11}$
6	$\frac{1}{5}$		$\frac{2}{6}$			$\frac{1}{3}$	
5				$\frac{3}{8}$			
4						$\frac{1}{2}$	
3		$\frac{3}{9}$			$\frac{1}{4}$		
2				$\frac{7}{12}$			
1							$\frac{3}{7}$
0	1	2	3	4	5	6	7

1. What is the sum of (0,6) and (4,7)?

2. What is the difference of (3,2) and (6,4)?

3. Which is greater: (3,2) or (2,6)?

4. What is the coordinate for $\frac{1}{4}$?

5. What is the sum of (7,7) and (5,6)?

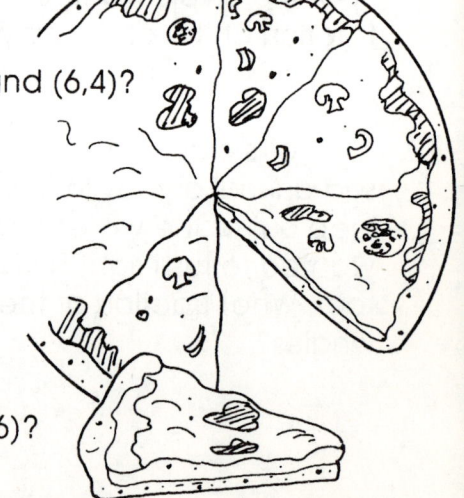

© 2006 Frank Schaffer Publications   0-88012-863-1

Using Coordinate Graphs

6. How much greater is (3,5) + (6,4) than (3,5) + (4,3)?

7. What is the difference of (6,4) and (4,7)?

8. What is the sum of (7,7) and (0,6)?

9. What is the difference of (3,2) and (5,6)?

10. Which is greater: (2,6) or (6,4)?

11. How much greater is (6,1) than (5,6)?

12. What is the sum of (4,3) and (2,6)?

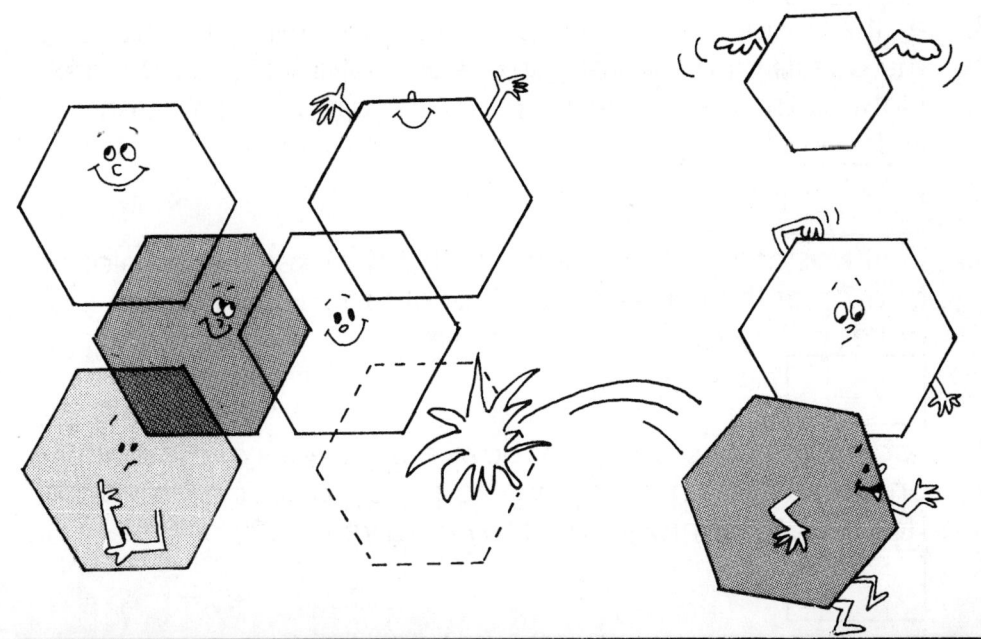

THERE'S MATH IN FOODS TOO!

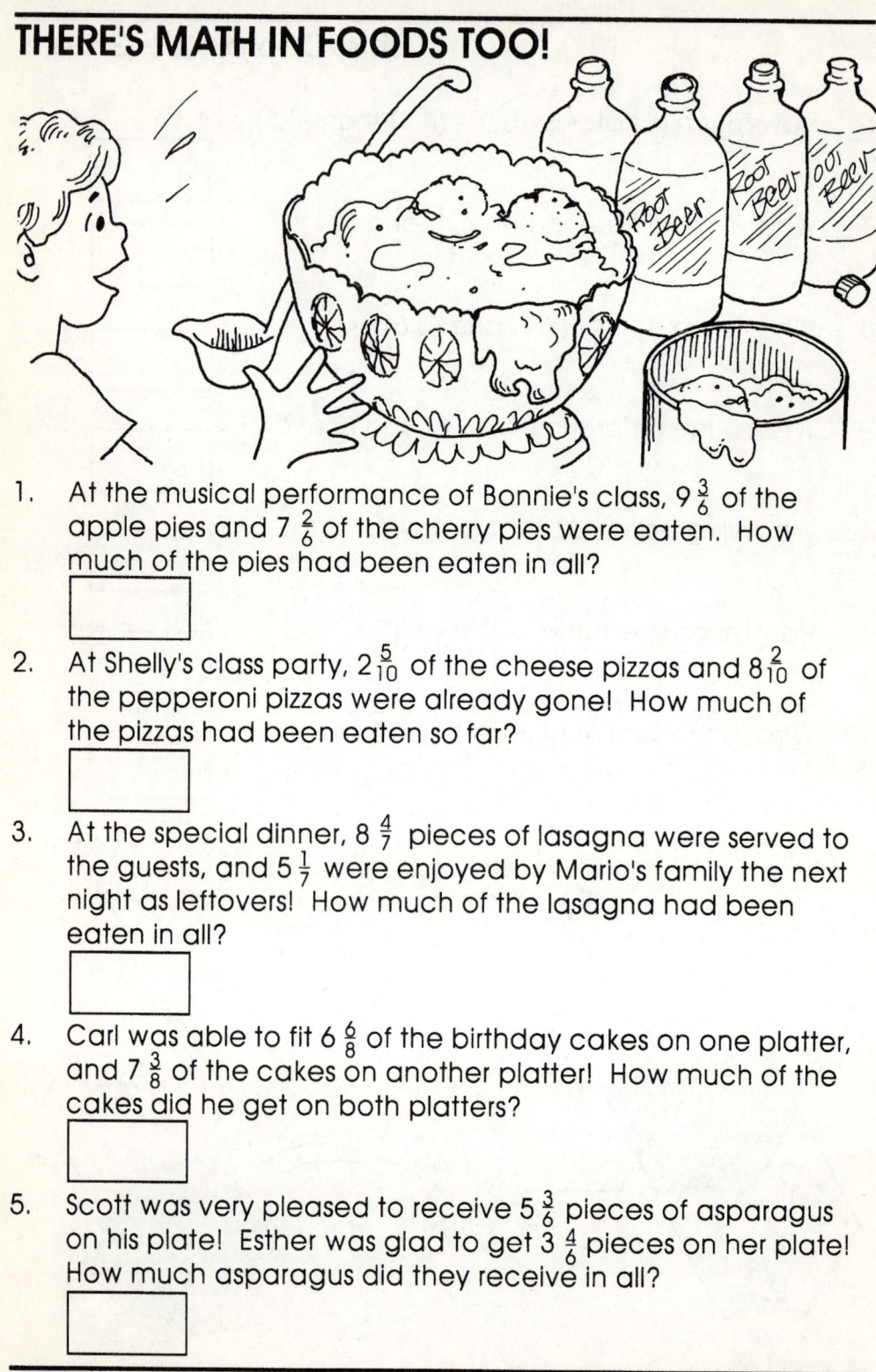

1. At the musical performance of Bonnie's class, $9\frac{3}{6}$ of the apple pies and $7\frac{2}{6}$ of the cherry pies were eaten. How much of the pies had been eaten in all?

2. At Shelly's class party, $2\frac{5}{10}$ of the cheese pizzas and $8\frac{2}{10}$ of the pepperoni pizzas were already gone! How much of the pizzas had been eaten so far?

3. At the special dinner, $8\frac{4}{7}$ pieces of lasagna were served to the guests, and $5\frac{1}{7}$ were enjoyed by Mario's family the next night as leftovers! How much of the lasagna had been eaten in all?

4. Carl was able to fit $6\frac{6}{8}$ of the birthday cakes on one platter, and $7\frac{3}{8}$ of the cakes on another platter! How much of the cakes did he get on both platters?

5. Scott was very pleased to receive $5\frac{3}{6}$ pieces of asparagus on his plate! Esther was glad to get $3\frac{4}{6}$ pieces on her plate! How much asparagus did they receive in all?

Addition of Mixed Numbers

6. Grant's doughnut statue was $1\frac{8}{10}$ meters high! Clayton's statue made of bakery delights was $1\frac{4}{10}$ meters high! How many meters high were both of them together?

7. Debbie's pretzel was $3\frac{1}{9}$ inches long unrolled. Camille's pretzel was $6\frac{7}{9}$ inches in length unrolled. How long were the pretzels together?

8. The letters of Roger's name were $8\frac{1}{4}$ cm tall. The letters of Gary's name were $8\frac{3}{4}$ cm tall. Both of them loved seeing their names on their birthday cakes! How many centimeters high were their names combined?

9. It took Lydia $4\frac{5}{12}$ eggs to make her cake right. It took Candace $9\frac{5}{12}$ eggs to make her cake the way she wanted it. How many eggs did they use in all?

10. Cyndi used $13\frac{2}{5}$ c of flour to make her special turkey pies! She also used $7\frac{3}{5}$ c of fresh carrots. How many cups of these two ingredients did she use?

11. Forrest put in $12\frac{1}{3}$ L of root beer into the punch bowl. Then he added $9\frac{1}{3}$ L of vanilla ice cream! How many liters of ingredients did he use to make this fabulous drink?

12. Brooke added $7\frac{2}{9}$ pt of strawberries to the ice cream mixture! Then she added $5\frac{8}{9}$ pt of bananas! How many pints of fruit did Brooke add to the homemade ice cream dessert?

© 2006 Frank Schaffer Publications   45   0-88012-863-1

HOW LONG, HOW TALL, HOW FAR?

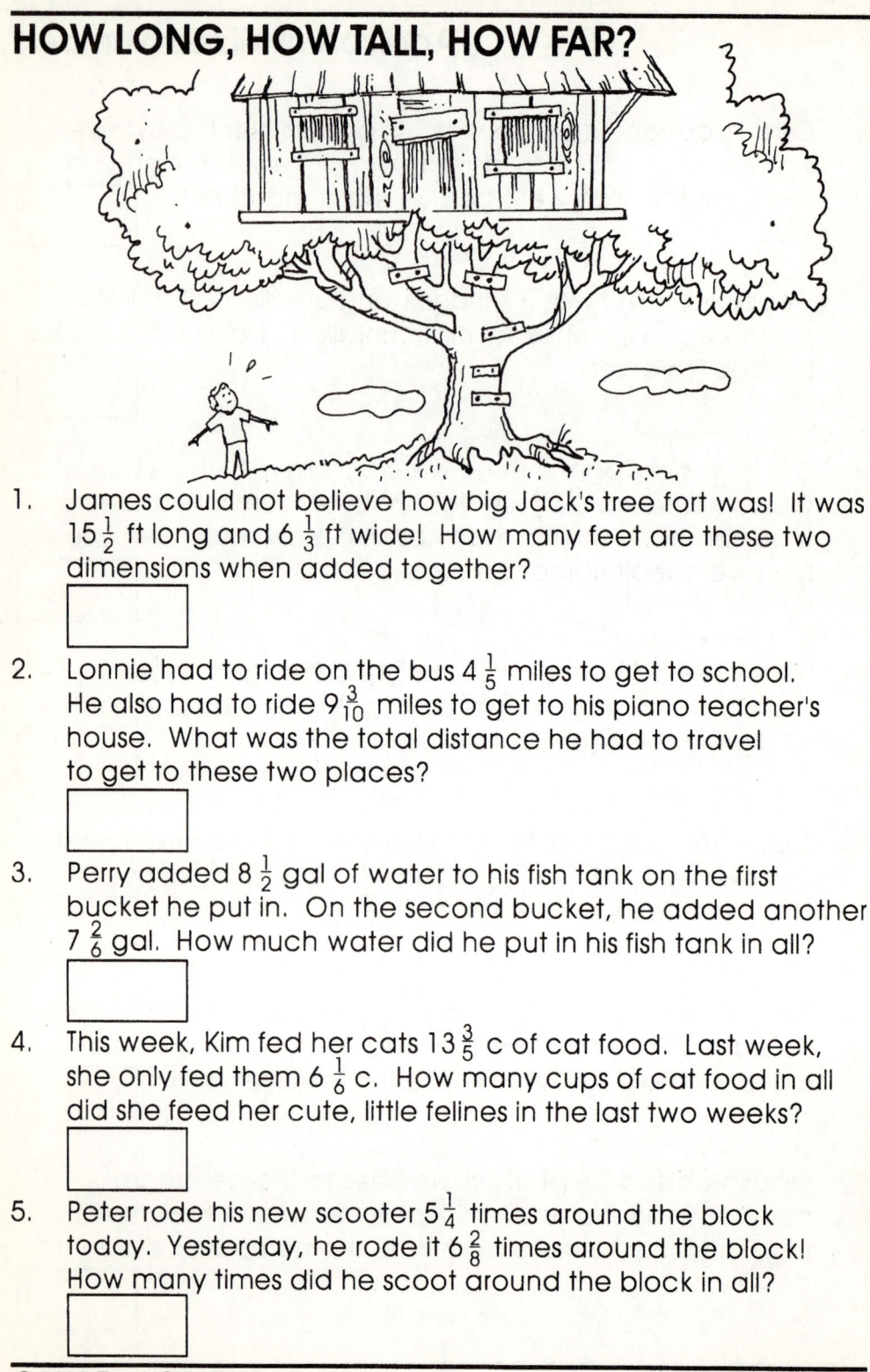

1. James could not believe how big Jack's tree fort was! It was $15\frac{1}{2}$ ft long and $6\frac{1}{3}$ ft wide! How many feet are these two dimensions when added together?

2. Lonnie had to ride on the bus $4\frac{1}{5}$ miles to get to school. He also had to ride $9\frac{3}{10}$ miles to get to his piano teacher's house. What was the total distance he had to travel to get to these two places?

3. Perry added $8\frac{1}{2}$ gal of water to his fish tank on the first bucket he put in. On the second bucket, he added another $7\frac{2}{6}$ gal. How much water did he put in his fish tank in all?

4. This week, Kim fed her cats $13\frac{3}{5}$ c of cat food. Last week, she only fed them $6\frac{1}{6}$ c. How many cups of cat food in all did she feed her cute, little felines in the last two weeks?

5. Peter rode his new scooter $5\frac{1}{4}$ times around the block today. Yesterday, he rode it $6\frac{2}{8}$ times around the block! How many times did he scoot around the block in all?

Addition of Mixed Numbers

6. Charles measured his piece of beef jerky to be $9\frac{1}{3}$ in. long. Cliff measured his piece to be $9\frac{3}{12}$ in. in length. How many inches were their pieces of beef jerky altogether?

7. Eric's turtle weighed $9\frac{2}{5}$ lb, and his brother's turtle weighed $7\frac{5}{15}$ lb. How many pounds did the turtles weigh in all?

8. The baby tegu lizards that Casey saw at the zoo were $12\frac{1}{6}$ in. long and $8\frac{4}{18}$ in. long. How long were they altogether?

9. Hershel could not believe that it only took him $6\frac{1}{2}$ min to swim across the lake! His friend Graham could not believe that it only took him $7\frac{2}{10}$ min to cross the lake! How many minutes altogether did it take them to cross the lake?

10. Sydel wove $2\frac{3}{7}$ ft of friendship rope last night while listening to her favorite music on the radio. Her friend Lynette was able to weave $5\frac{3}{14}$ ft of friendship rope when she got home from school. How many feet of rope did they weave in all?

11. Christina's hair was $8\frac{1}{5}$ in. long after she got a haircut. She measured it 2 months later and found out that it grew another $1\frac{1}{2}$ in! How long is her hair now?

12. Kelly could not believe how tall the stalks of corn in her garden were! One was $6\frac{4}{12}$ in. tall, and the other was $7\frac{1}{2}$ in. tall! How high did the stalks reach for the sky in all?

LET'S GET INTO SPORTS!

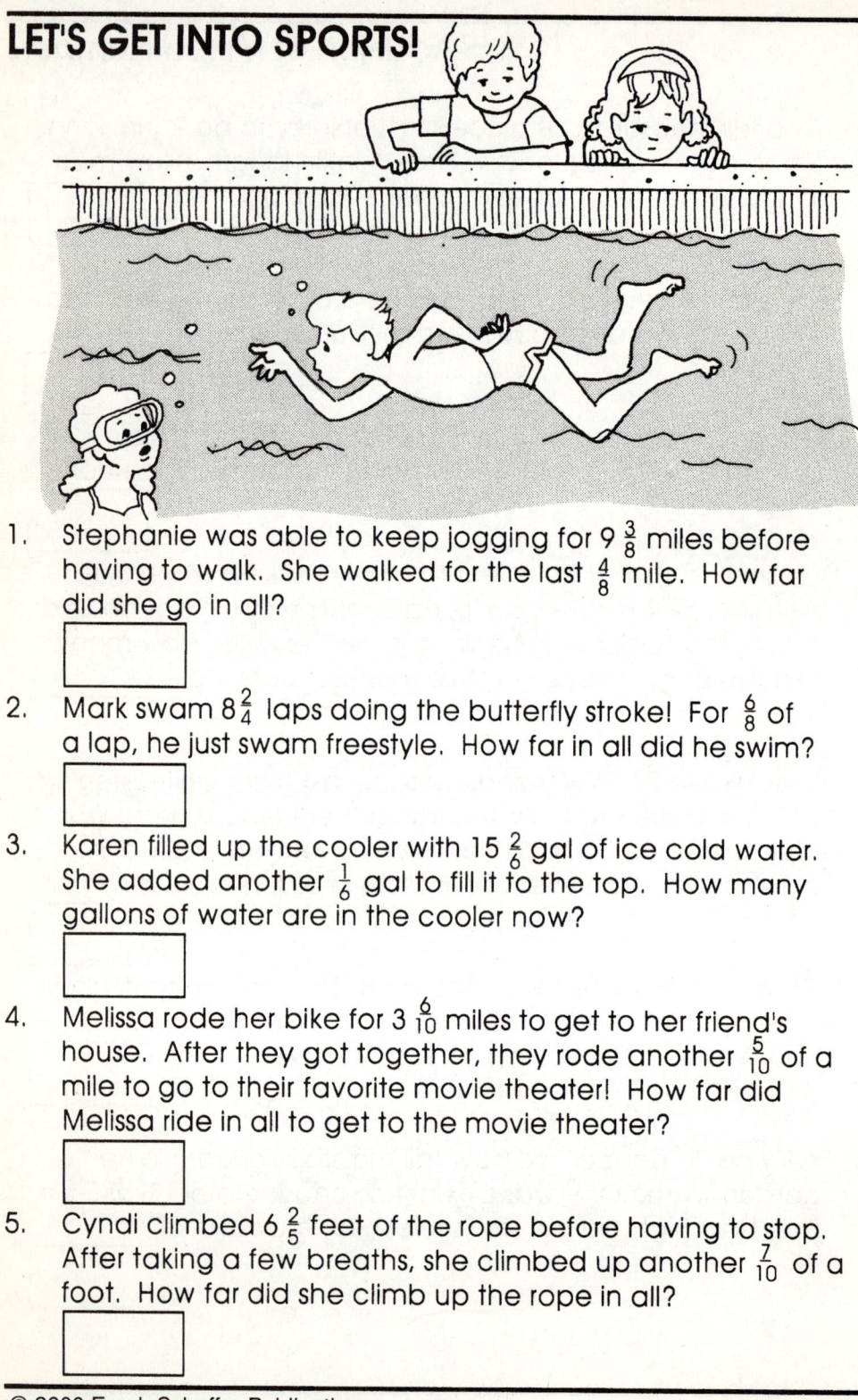

1. Stephanie was able to keep jogging for $9\frac{3}{8}$ miles before having to walk. She walked for the last $\frac{4}{8}$ mile. How far did she go in all?

2. Mark swam $8\frac{2}{4}$ laps doing the butterfly stroke! For $\frac{6}{8}$ of a lap, he just swam freestyle. How far in all did he swim?

3. Karen filled up the cooler with $15\frac{2}{6}$ gal of ice cold water. She added another $\frac{1}{6}$ gal to fill it to the top. How many gallons of water are in the cooler now?

4. Melissa rode her bike for $3\frac{6}{10}$ miles to get to her friend's house. After they got together, they rode another $\frac{5}{10}$ of a mile to go to their favorite movie theater! How far did Melissa ride in all to get to the movie theater?

5. Cyndi climbed $6\frac{2}{5}$ feet of the rope before having to stop. After taking a few breaths, she climbed up another $\frac{7}{10}$ of a foot. How far did she climb up the rope in all?

© 2006 Frank Schaffer Publications

Addition of Mixed Numbers

6. Viola could not believe that she could jump $5\frac{7}{10}$ ft into the air on the trampoline. On her next try, she added another $\frac{3}{5}$ of a foot! How far did she jump on the second try?

7. Laurie walked $7\frac{2}{6}$ miles for the walkathon before she thought she would drop right in her tracks! After a brief rest, she got up and walked another $\frac{2}{3}$ mile. How far did she walk in all?

8. Grant was able to swim under water for $3\frac{5}{7}$ laps without coming up for a breath! His friends were impressed! The next time, he went another $\frac{6}{14}$ of a lap farther! How far did he go under water on the second try?

9. Tricia lifted $5\frac{3}{8}$ lb of heavy weights over her head! She stopped and added another $\frac{1}{4}$ of a pound. How many pounds of weights could she lift over her head now?

10. Dale jumped $5\frac{3}{6}$ ft on his first try at the running long jump. On his second try, he jumped another $\frac{7}{12}$ of a foot. How many feet did he jump on the second try?

11. Trevor, after much practice, was able to clear $4\frac{1}{3}$ ft on the high jump! But, he didn't want to stop just yet! He had the coach add another $\frac{3}{6}$ of a foot to the height of the pole. How many feet would he have to clear now?

12. Duane was able to run to the store and back in $14\frac{3}{7}$ min. He tried running again without a rest and only added another $\frac{6}{21}$ of a minute onto his time. How fast did he run to the store and back the second time?

AREN'T REPTILES JUST THE CUTEST THINGS?

1. Mattie's gecko measured $11\frac{3}{4}$ in. long. Her brother's gecko measured $9\frac{1}{4}$ in. long. How much longer was Mattie's gecko? I wonder whose barked the loudest!

2. Lynn's race runner lizard was $6\frac{6}{8}$ in. long. Her baby green lizard was $3\frac{4}{8}$ in. long. How much longer was her race runner lizard?

3. Sandy's skink was $10\frac{3}{5}$ in. long. Her sandfish was $7\frac{1}{5}$ in. long. How much longer was her skink?

4. Sean's flap-necked chameleon was $12\frac{3}{4}$ in. long. His body alone was $6\frac{1}{4}$ in. long. How long was his tail?

5. Weslie's pet soa-soa water dragon looked just like a dinosaur! It was $17\frac{2}{3}$ in. long! I guess he was a little small for a dinosaur, don't you think? His tail alone was $9\frac{1}{3}$ in. long. How long was his body?

Subtraction of Mixed Numbers

6. Martha's baby basilisk lizard was the greenest lizard any of her friends had ever seen! It was $11\frac{1}{12}$ in. long. I'm not sure if she knew that it would soon grow to be $31\frac{9}{12}$ in. long! How many more inches did it have to grow?

7. Sarah's pretty blue-collared lizard was a total of $9\frac{7}{10}$ in. long. Her Texas horned lizard was $7\frac{3}{10}$ in. long. How much longer was her collared lizard?

8. Eric's spiny, soft-shelled turtle was $15\frac{6}{7}$ in. long. His young matamata was $9\frac{2}{7}$ in. long. What an incredible-looking animal! How much longer was his spiny, soft-shelled turtle?

9. Allen had two murray river turtles. One was $11\frac{5}{9}$ in. long, and the other was $8\frac{2}{9}$ in. long. What is the difference in their lengths?

10. Alex's alligator snapping turtle was only $7\frac{4}{5}$ in. long. It had a ways to go before it was full grown. It was only $5\frac{2}{5}$ in. long when he first got it. How many inches had it grown since he first brought it home?

11. Darren's gopher tortoise was $13\frac{8}{9}$ in. long. His wood turtle was $8\frac{3}{9}$ in. in length. How much longer was his gopher tortoise?

12. Andy's slowworm was $14\frac{5}{8}$ in. long. His California legless lizard was only $6\frac{2}{8}$ in. long. How much longer was his slowworm?

HEAD 'EM UP, IT'S TIME TO HIKE!

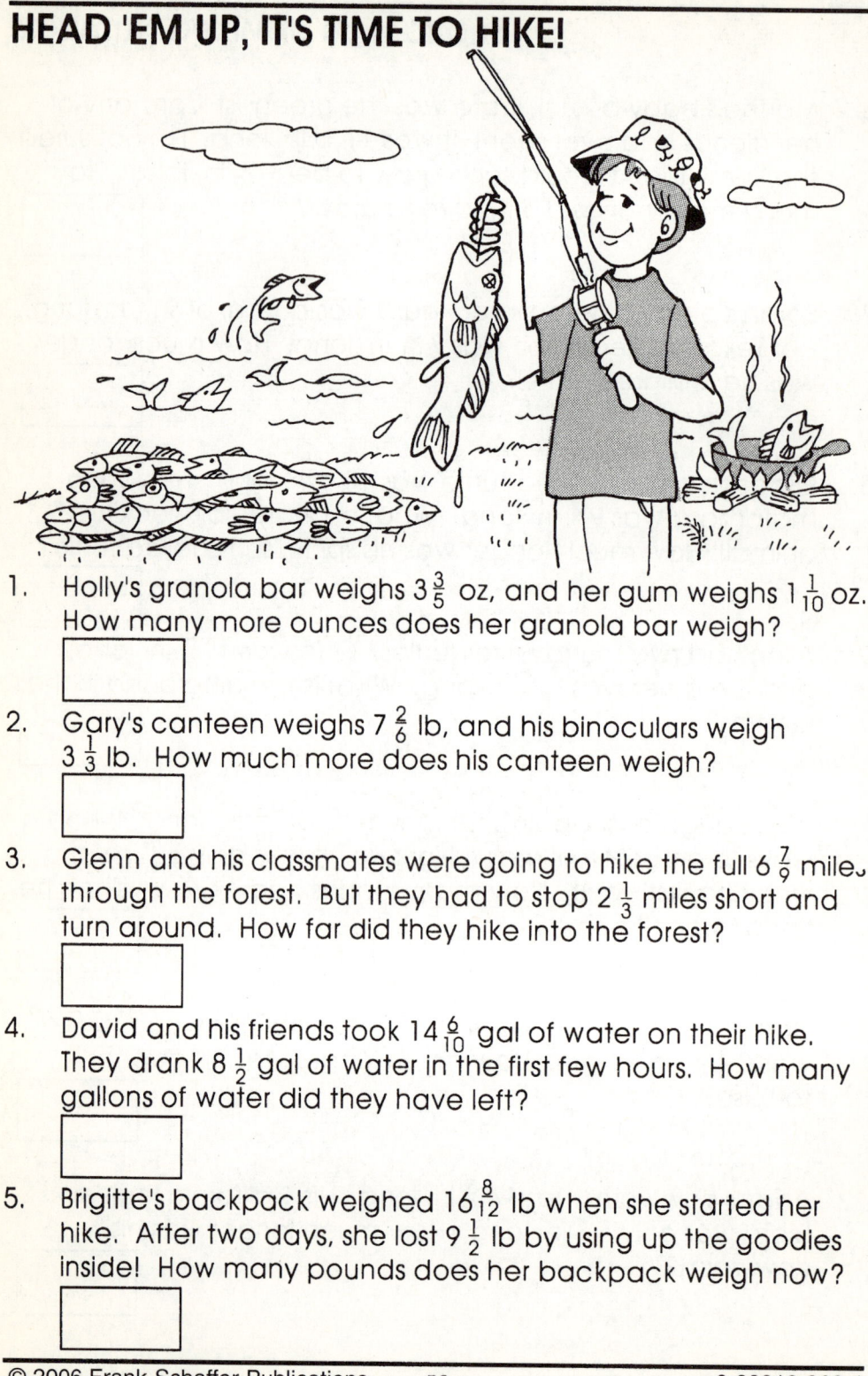

1. Holly's granola bar weighs $3\frac{3}{5}$ oz, and her gum weighs $1\frac{1}{10}$ oz. How many more ounces does her granola bar weigh?

2. Gary's canteen weighs $7\frac{2}{6}$ lb, and his binoculars weigh $3\frac{1}{3}$ lb. How much more does his canteen weigh?

3. Glenn and his classmates were going to hike the full $6\frac{7}{9}$ miles through the forest. But they had to stop $2\frac{1}{3}$ miles short and turn around. How far did they hike into the forest?

4. David and his friends took $14\frac{6}{10}$ gal of water on their hike. They drank $8\frac{1}{2}$ gal of water in the first few hours. How many gallons of water did they have left?

5. Brigitte's backpack weighed $16\frac{8}{12}$ lb when she started her hike. After two days, she lost $9\frac{1}{2}$ lb by using up the goodies inside! How many pounds does her backpack weigh now?

© 2006 Frank Schaffer Publications

Subtraction of Mixed Numbers

6. Claire and her classmates had planned to hike a total of $12\frac{10}{20}$ miles in the week that they were camping. After a lot of sore feet, they decided to limit it to $7\frac{2}{10}$ miles. How many miles did they shave off their trip?

7. Daniel started out with $13\frac{8}{15}$ lb in his backpack. But after careful pondering and decisive moves to lighten it, he eliminated $7\frac{1}{5}$ lb! How many pounds did his backpack weigh after he got rid of some of the weight?

8. Earl's fishing group caught a total of $14\frac{3}{6}$ lb of fish. The group cooked up $9\frac{1}{2}$ lb the first day back from its trip. How many pounds of fish were left to enjoy?

9. Altogether Paul's class found and kept $18\frac{6}{7}$ lb of rocks. The students decided the rocks were getting too heavy, so they put back $9\frac{2}{14}$ lb. How many pounds did they end up keeping?

10. Gary picked $9\frac{5}{8}$ lb of fruit on his hike! But he ate $5\frac{4}{16}$ lb coming back! How much fruit did he have left when he got back?

11. Charlie could not believe that his backpack weighed an extra $6\frac{5}{7}$ lb after getting wet in the rain! After it dried in the sun, it lost $3\frac{2}{21}$ lb. How many more pounds did the backpack have to lose to return to its original weight?

HOW FAR IS IT GOING TO BE?

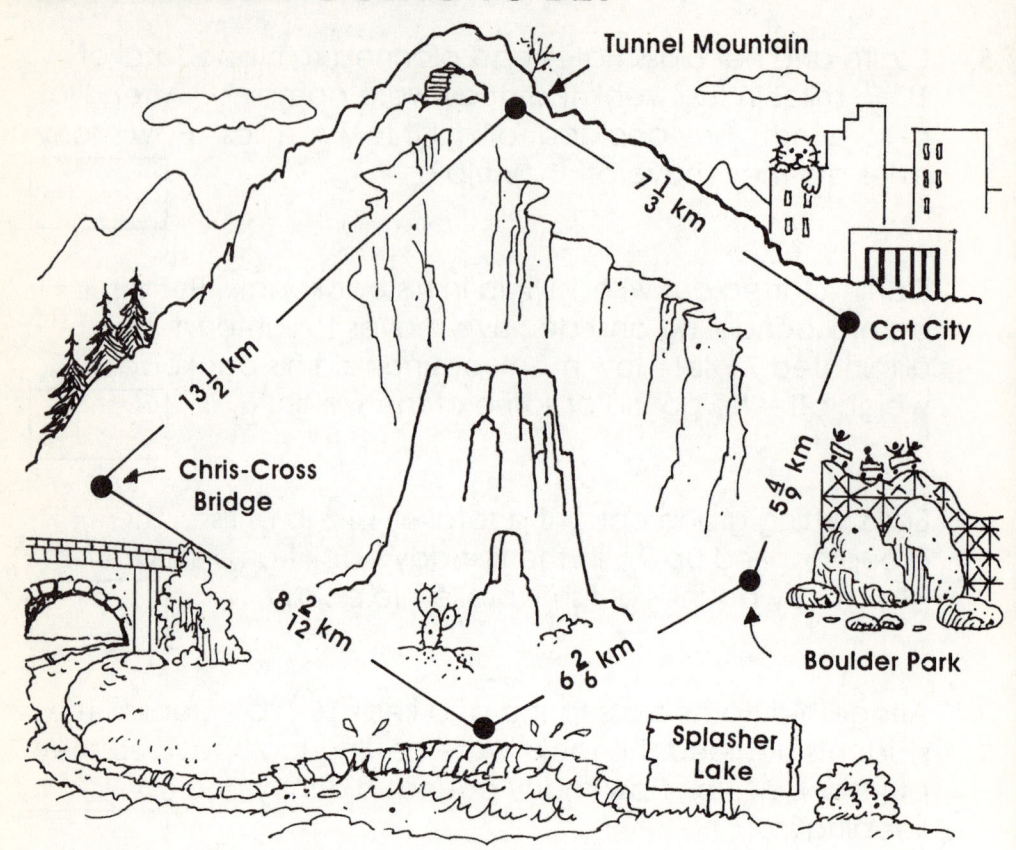

Distances shown on map:
- Tunnel Mountain to Cat City: $7\frac{1}{3}$ km
- Chris-Cross Bridge to Tunnel Mountain: $13\frac{1}{2}$ km
- Cat City to Boulder Park: $5\frac{9}{6}$ km
- Chris-Cross Bridge to Splasher Lake: $8\frac{2}{12}$ km
- Splasher Lake to Boulder Park: $6\frac{2}{6}$ km

1. How much farther is it from Chris-Cross Bridge to Splasher Lake than from Splasher Lake to Boulder Park?

2. How many kilometers is it to travel from Tunnel Mountain to Boulder Park, passing through Cat City?

3. How far it is it to travel from Chris-Cross Bridge to Cat City passing through Tunnel Mountain?

4. How far is it to travel from Splasher Lake to Cat City passing through Boulder Park?

Using a Map

5. How many kilometers is it from Tunnel Mountain to Splasher Lake passing over Chris-Cross Bridge?

6. How much farther is it to travel from Chris-Cross Bridge to Tunnel Mountain than it is to travel from Chris-Cross Bridge to Splasher Lake?

7. How far is the shortest route from Chris-Cross Bridge to Boulder Park?

8. What is the difference to travel from Chris-Cross Bridge to Tunnel Mountain as compared to traveling from Tunnel Mountain to Cat City?

9. Which is the shortest route from Tunnel Mountain to Splasher Lake?

10. Which route starting at Boulder Park is a distance of $12\frac{7}{9}$ kilometers?

11. Which is the shortest route from Cat City to Chris-Cross Bridge?

12. Here's a real challenge to prove how smart you are! Can you figure out how far you would travel if you started at Tunnel Mountain, crossed through all the landmarks and ended up back at Tunnel Mountain?

ART IS SUCH A GREAT WAY TO EXPRESS YOURSELF!

1. Wendy was helping to draw a title for the yearbook page that her class was designing. It started out $5\frac{6}{7}$ inches long. She shortened it by $\frac{2}{7}$ of an inch. How long is it now?

2. Rochelle added $3\frac{5}{8}$ cups of flour to her famous cookie recipe. Realizing she had a tad too much, she scooped out $\frac{1}{4}$ of a cup. How many cups of flour did she end up putting in her cookie batter?

3. Kevin's ceramic bowl was $6\frac{6}{10}$ inches in diameter. After looking it over, he decided to narrow it by $\frac{4}{10}$ of an inch. What is the diameter of his bowl now?

4. Pam's drawing was $9\frac{3}{7}$ inches wide. But, in order to make it fit nicely into the picture frame, she had to trim off $\frac{1}{21}$ of an inch. What is the width of her drawing now?

5. Suzanne's bean mosaic was only $2\frac{6}{15}$ inches wide. She decided to trim off $\frac{1}{5}$ of an inch on one side. How wide is this miniature mosaic now?

Subtraction of Mixed Numbers

6. Gabriel poured $7\frac{8}{12}$ cups of water into his mixture of plaster of Paris. When he saw that it was just a little too much, he drained off $\frac{6}{12}$ of a cup. How much water did he end up adding?

7. Sophia had woven a colorful friendship bracelet that was $10\frac{2}{3}$ inches long. She felt that it was just a tiny bit too long and trimmed off $\frac{1}{6}$ of an inch. How long is her bracelet now?

8. Carmen's papier-mâché planet started out being $5\frac{2}{5}$ inches in diameter. After it dried, it shrunk $\frac{1}{10}$ of an inch. What was the diameter of his planet after it dried?

9. Cheryl placed $2\frac{5}{6}$ oz of colored ink on the plate for her spin art project. Just before she started it up, she took off $\frac{3}{6}$ of an ounce, thinking that it was too much! How many ounces of ink did she end up using?

10. Joni carefully placed $4\frac{3}{8}$ lb of clay on her potter's wheel. She immediately carved off $\frac{1}{4}$ of a pound and placed it on the table by her side. How much clay did she have on her wheel?

11. Tiffany started out with $3\frac{5}{10}$ oz of miniature beads to make her bracelet. She saw that her friend didn't quite have enough and immediately gave her $\frac{1}{2}$ of an ounce of beads. How many ounces of beads did she end up using?

12. Bill's family animal collage was originally $8\frac{6}{8}$ in. wide. He trimmed off $\frac{1}{8}$ of an inch from one side to even it out. How wide is it now?

CAN YOU REALLY TAKE A "PART" OF SOMETHING FROM A "WHOLE" OF SOMETHING?

1. Lionel squeezed 6 cups of fresh orange juice to share with his family! He scooped out $\frac{3}{8}$ of a cup of seeds. How many cups of juice did he end up with?

2. Murray tried to fit 12 oz of ice water into his canteen. He had to pour out $\frac{1}{2}$ of an ounce to get the lid on without spilling the water. How much water was he able to fit in his canteen?

3. Lowell had 3 lb of pomegranates to share with his friends as an after-school snack. Lowell enjoyed $\frac{2}{4}$ of a pound and gave the rest to his friends. How many pounds of this delicious fruit did he give to his friends to enjoy?

4. Stacy put 8 oz of cat food in her kitty's dish. When the cat was finished eating, there was $\frac{3}{11}$ of an ounce of food left in the dish. How many ounces did Stacy's cat eat in all?

5. Royal bought 5 lb of black seedless grapes to have in his lunches. He took $\frac{3}{7}$ of a pound with him the first day. How many pounds did he have left for the rest of the week?

Subtraction of Fractions

6. Tracy started to drink her 12 oz glass of milk when she happened to glance down and see her cute, little snowball kitten peeking up at her. She poured $\frac{7}{9}$ of an ounce of milk in a little bowl for her kitten. How many ounces of milk did she end up drinking herself?

7. Tricia picked 7 baskets of apricots while visiting her cousin's farm. Since some of the apricots were overripe, $\frac{2}{5}$ of a basket had to be thrown away. How many baskets did Tricia take home with her?

8. Adam bought 14 lb of dog food for his faithful, little tail-wagger! He poured $\frac{3}{12}$ of a pound into the doggie bowl as soon as he arrived home. How many pounds were left in the bag?

9. Linda made a 9 oz banana-milk drink in the blender. Bananas made up $\frac{2}{6}$ of an ounce of the drink. How many ounces of the drink was made with milk?

10. Mark picked out 15 cans of tuna fish while shopping with his mom at the grocery store. As soon as he got home, he made a tuna fish sandwich and used $\frac{6}{10}$ of a can on his bread. How many cans of tuna fish were left?

11. Pamela's family purchased $\frac{3}{15}$ of a pound short of 20 lb of watermelon for its family picnic on Saturday. How many pounds of watermelon were bought?

IF YOU'VE GOT A CHOICE, PICK SCIENCE!

1. In David's class, $\frac{3}{5}$ of the boys built model rockets to launch. Streamers were used on $\frac{2}{9}$ of the rockets to slow them down instead of parachutes. What fraction of the boys built rockets that had streamers?

2. In Heather's class, $\frac{1}{8}$ of the students wanted to help build the huge papier-mâché volcano! Of the students that helped, $\frac{6}{7}$ got covered in papier-mâché mess. What fraction of the students got all messy?

3. On Saturday, $\frac{2}{8}$ of Debbie's class volunteered to help clean the park grounds to help get them ready for the big science show! Can you believe that $\frac{3}{4}$ of the class stayed all day to help! Wasn't that thoughtful? What fraction of the class was able to stay all day?

4. A total of $\frac{9}{12}$ of the boys in Mark's scout troop built and designed their own skateboards. $\frac{2}{4}$ of these skateboards were built with oak. What fraction of the scouts made skateboards using oak?

Multiplication of Fractions

5. At Clifford's school, $\frac{3}{9}$ of the students wanted to learn about the new science museum that was just built. This month, $\frac{1}{5}$ of the students were able to go see it. What fraction of students were able to go see it right away?

6. Lots of people came to watch the space shuttle land. Of these people, $\frac{2}{7}$ were students from California and $\frac{6}{8}$ of the students were fifth graders! What fraction of the students were fifth graders?

7. Making fossils out of plaster of Paris is fun. That's why $\frac{5}{10}$ of Matthew's class chose to make them. Only $\frac{3}{6}$ of these students used shells to make their imprints in their plaster. What fraction of the class used shells?

8. On Saturday, $\frac{5}{8}$ of Peter's class came to school to learn how to make solar ovens. Pizzas were cooked by $\frac{2}{5}$ of the students who came. What fraction of the class chose to cook pizza?

9. Cecilia used $\frac{3}{7}$ of her balloons to learn about static electricity by rubbing them on her head and sticking them to things. After lunch, $\frac{3}{4}$ of the balloons were still sticking on the wall! What fraction were still sticking to the wall?

10. For the hot air balloon demonstrations and rides on Saturday, $\frac{6}{7}$ of Curt's class attended. Can you believe that $\frac{5}{7}$ of the students were brave enough to want to ride in the balloons? What fraction of the class wanted to take a ride?

IT'S TIME TO PACK YOUR TENT!

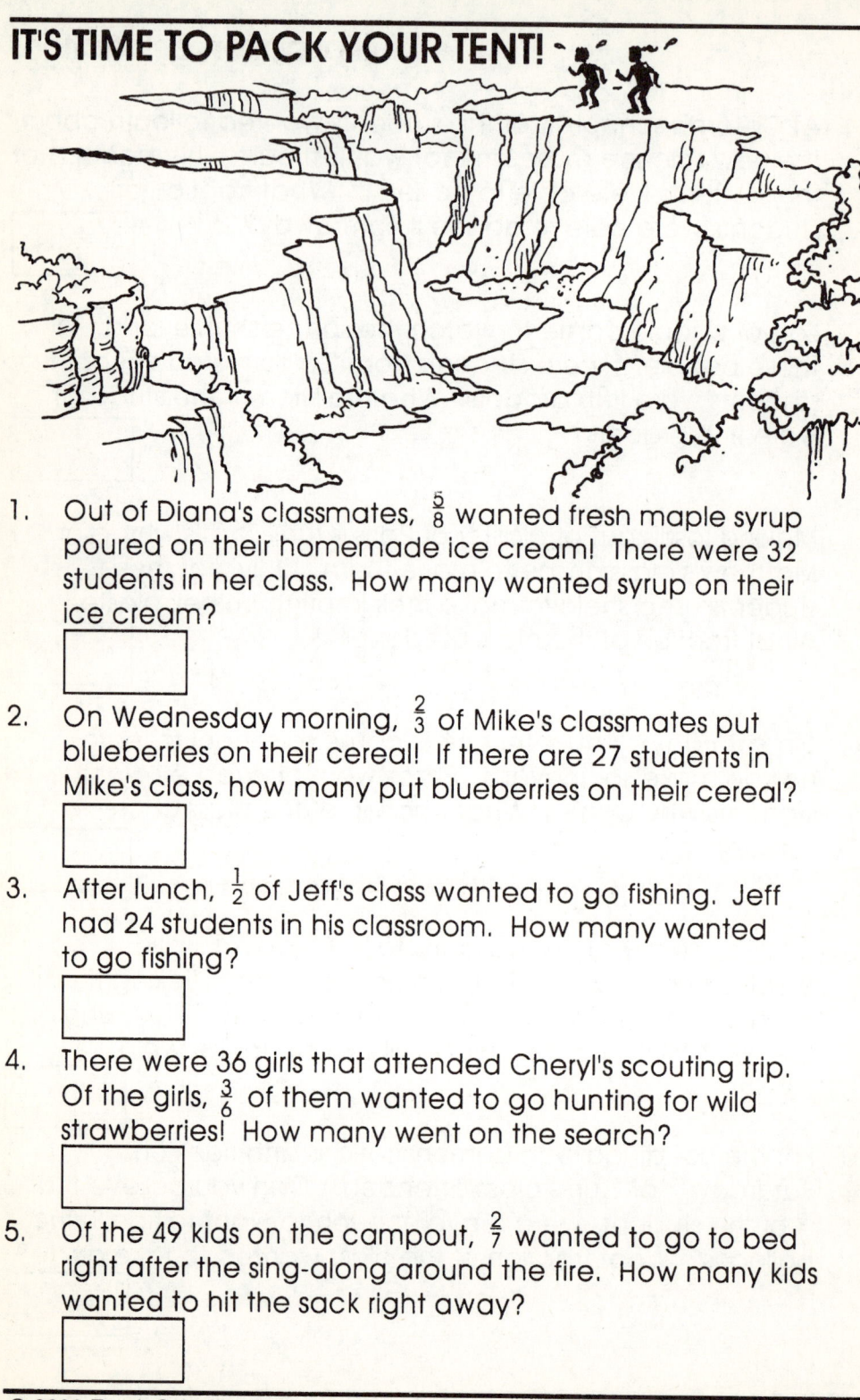

1. Out of Diana's classmates, $\frac{5}{8}$ wanted fresh maple syrup poured on their homemade ice cream! There were 32 students in her class. How many wanted syrup on their ice cream?

2. On Wednesday morning, $\frac{2}{3}$ of Mike's classmates put blueberries on their cereal! If there are 27 students in Mike's class, how many put blueberries on their cereal?

3. After lunch, $\frac{1}{2}$ of Jeff's class wanted to go fishing. Jeff had 24 students in his classroom. How many wanted to go fishing?

4. There were 36 girls that attended Cheryl's scouting trip. Of the girls, $\frac{3}{6}$ of them wanted to go hunting for wild strawberries! How many went on the search?

5. Of the 49 kids on the campout, $\frac{2}{7}$ wanted to go to bed right after the sing-along around the fire. How many kids wanted to hit the sack right away?

Multiplication of Fractions

6. Out of the 18 campers, $\frac{1}{9}$ used water to make soup their first night out. How many campers made soup with water?

7. Making biscuits over the open fire looked like so much fun that $\frac{5}{6}$ of the 24 campers wanted to learn how. How many campers learned how to make biscuits?

8. Since the water in the campers' canteens was not very cold, $\frac{7}{8}$ of the campers wanted ice. If there were 16 campers, how many wanted ice for their canteens?

9. Of the 25 students in Whitney's class, $\frac{3}{5}$ wanted to have fresh blackberries on top of their cereal. How fortunate they were to find the wild berries near their campsite! How many students wanted these wild berries?

10. 48 students from Andy's class went on the overnight. When it was time to hunt for geodes, $\frac{2}{8}$ of the students wanted to stay behind. How many students wanted to stay behind in all?

11. A total of 36 campers attended the trip to the lake. The water looked so inviting that $\frac{2}{12}$ of the campers wanted to go swimming right away! How many wanted to get in the water as soon as possible?

12. The hike to the canyon looked so difficult that only $\frac{5}{11}$ of the 44 campers from Donna's scouting group went. How many hiked to the canyon in all?

© 2006 Frank Schaffer Publications　　　　0-88012-863-1

MULTIPLYING MIXED NUMBERS WILL NOT MIX YOU UP!

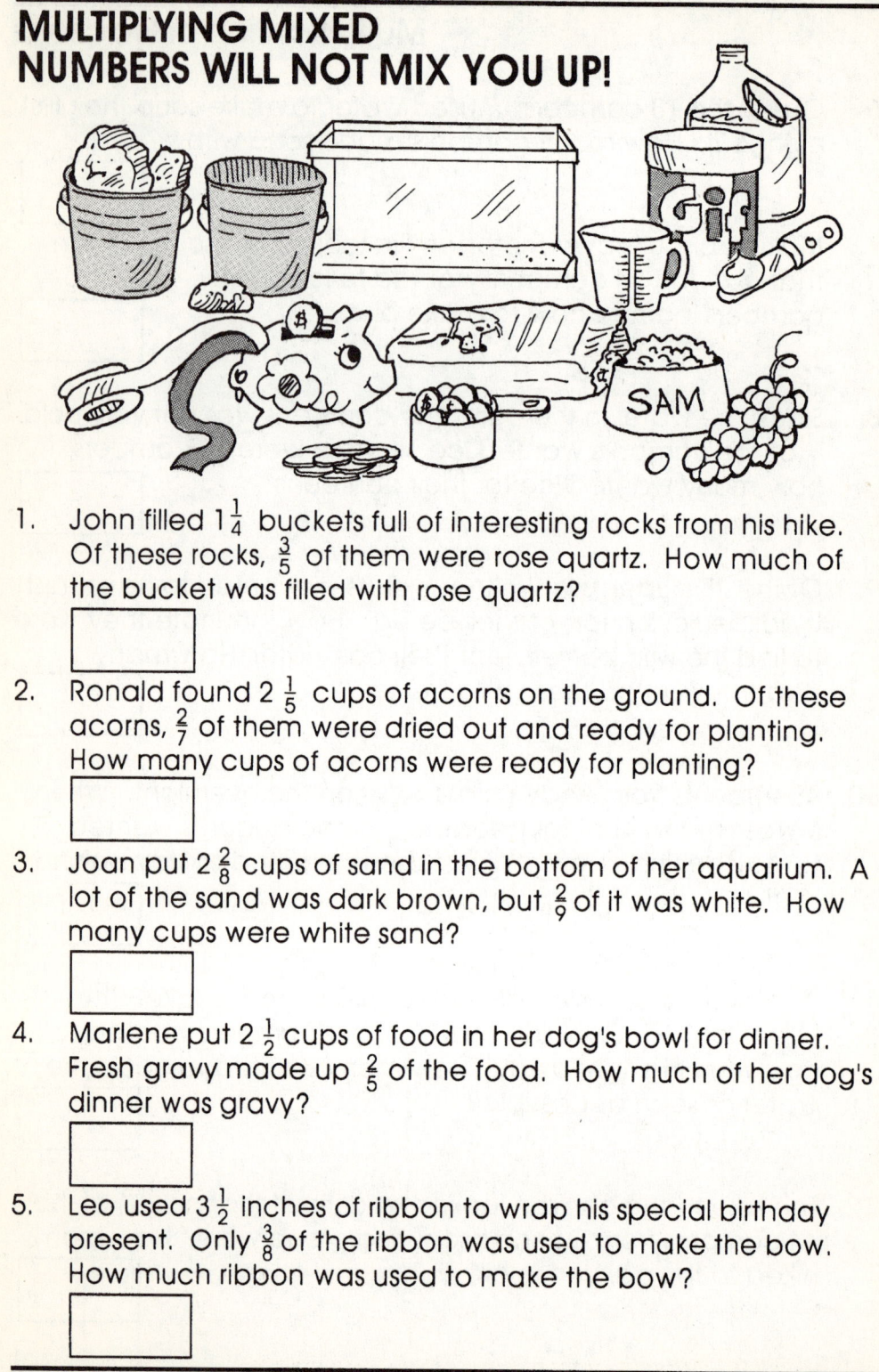

1. John filled $1\frac{1}{4}$ buckets full of interesting rocks from his hike. Of these rocks, $\frac{3}{5}$ of them were rose quartz. How much of the bucket was filled with rose quartz?

2. Ronald found $2\frac{1}{5}$ cups of acorns on the ground. Of these acorns, $\frac{2}{7}$ of them were dried out and ready for planting. How many cups of acorns were ready for planting?

3. Joan put $2\frac{2}{8}$ cups of sand in the bottom of her aquarium. A lot of the sand was dark brown, but $\frac{2}{9}$ of it was white. How many cups were white sand?

4. Marlene put $2\frac{1}{2}$ cups of food in her dog's bowl for dinner. Fresh gravy made up $\frac{2}{5}$ of the food. How much of her dog's dinner was gravy?

5. Leo used $3\frac{1}{2}$ inches of ribbon to wrap his special birthday present. Only $\frac{3}{8}$ of the ribbon was used to make the bow. How much ribbon was used to make the bow?

© 2006 Frank Schaffer Publications   0-88012-863-1

Multiplication of Mixed Numbers

6. Kimiko put $1\frac{1}{9}$ cups of salt into the jar full of water to make salt crystals. Only $\frac{1}{8}$ of the salt would not mix with the water solution. How much of the salt did not mix with the water after the solution became saturated?

7. Kay bought $2\frac{1}{6}$ lb of grapes at the store. She put $\frac{3}{5}$ of them out in the sun on a special tray to make her own raisins! How many pounds of raisins did she make?

8. Daniel put $2\frac{2}{3}$ gal of water into his fish tank. Then he decided to remove $\frac{1}{3}$ of the water. How many gallons of water did he remove?

9. Janet put $2\frac{1}{5}$ oz of peanut butter into her cookie mix. She scooped out $\frac{3}{7}$ of it when she realized that it looked like too much. How many ounces of peanut butter did she scoop out?

10. Julius filled up his piggy bank with $1\frac{2}{9}$ cups of coins. If $\frac{3}{5}$ of the coins were dimes, how much of the bank was filled with dimes?

11. There were $2\frac{1}{6}$ gal of water left in the water cooler when Dixie woke up. After her dad and brother finished mowing the yard, they drank $\frac{3}{8}$ of the water. How many gallons of water did they drink?

LET'S MEASURE IT AND THEN MAKE IT!

1. Francisco cut 5 pieces of wood into $1\frac{2}{3}$ ft lengths each. How many feet does this equal in all?

2. Todd used two $1\frac{1}{4}$ ft long pieces of plastic to make his colorful book cover. How many feet was the plastic in all?

3. Gary used 3 pieces of nylon string to weave his rope. Each piece was $3\frac{1}{4}$ feet long. How long were the strings altogether?

4. Nine students in Alex's class each used a piece of balsa wood $2\frac{1}{6}$ ft long to make their airplanes. How many feet of balsa wood did the class use in all?

5. Each of Carolyn's 2 pieces of leather were $3\frac{1}{6}$ inches long. How long were they altogether?

Multiplication of Fractions

6. Each of the 4 branches that Cheryl was going to use for the macramé was $5\frac{1}{2}$ feet long. How long were they in all?

7. Each of the 7 pieces of plywood that Bill was going to use for his tree fort was $1\frac{1}{5}$ feet long. How long were the pieces of wood altogether?

8. Both of the rocks that Sarah was going to use to make her necklace were $1\frac{1}{3}$ inches long. How long were they in all?

9. Each of the 8 pieces of felt that Shelly was using to decorate her puppets with was $2\frac{1}{7}$ inches wide. How wide in all was the felt that she was using?

10. Five times Christina added $1\frac{1}{9}$ cups of flour to make her pizza dough. How much dough did she use in all?

11. Each of the 3 designs that Steven cut out was $2\frac{1}{5}$ feet in diameter. How many feet in diameter were they altogether?

12. Michelle used 6 bolts that were each $1\frac{2}{7}$ inches long to fasten her wood project together. What was the total length of the bolts?

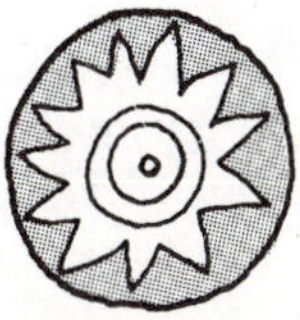

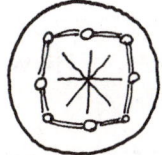

FOOD AND DIVISION WERE MEANT FOR EACH OTHER!

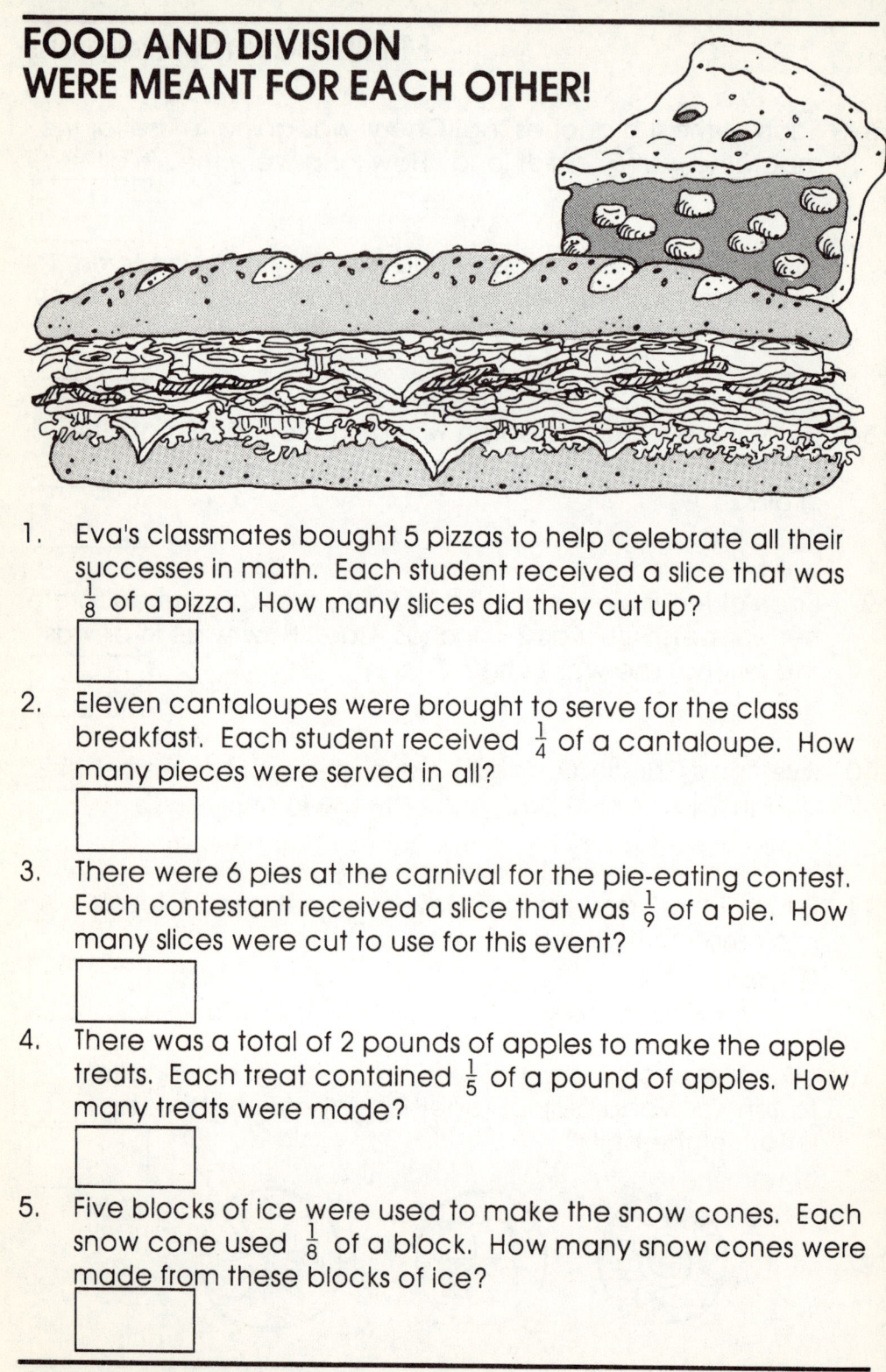

1. Eva's classmates bought 5 pizzas to help celebrate all their successes in math. Each student received a slice that was $\frac{1}{8}$ of a pizza. How many slices did they cut up?

2. Eleven cantaloupes were brought to serve for the class breakfast. Each student received $\frac{1}{4}$ of a cantaloupe. How many pieces were served in all?

3. There were 6 pies at the carnival for the pie-eating contest. Each contestant received a slice that was $\frac{1}{9}$ of a pie. How many slices were cut to use for this event?

4. There was a total of 2 pounds of apples to make the apple treats. Each treat contained $\frac{1}{5}$ of a pound of apples. How many treats were made?

5. Five blocks of ice were used to make the snow cones. Each snow cone used $\frac{1}{8}$ of a block. How many snow cones were made from these blocks of ice?

Division of Fractions

6. Richard's dad bought 7 bottles of mineral water to drink at the park. Each cup that he drank held $\frac{1}{7}$ of a bottle. How many cups was he able to drink?

7. There were 3 small cakes at Roger's birthday party. Each child received a piece that was $\frac{2}{6}$ of one cake. How many children attended Roger's birthday party in all?

8. Eight watermelons were brought to the family picnic and sliced. Each slice was $\frac{1}{7}$ of a watermelon. How many slices were served?

9. Earl's mom and dad bought 4 submarine sandwiches and divided them into pieces. Each piece was $\frac{1}{6}$ of a sandwich. How many pieces did they make after cutting up the sandwiches?

10. Six stalks of celery were used to make the "bumps on a log" treats. Each treat was made with $\frac{1}{3}$ of a stalk of celery. How many treats were made in all?

11. Two bottles of ketchup were brought to put on the hamburgers at Samuel's party. On each child's burger, $\frac{1}{7}$ of a bottle was used. How many burgers were served at his party?

12. Four containers of milk were brought to serve cereal with. Each student had $\frac{1}{5}$ of a container poured on top of his/her cereal. How many students did this milk serve?

HERE'S A CHANCE TO PROVE YOURSELF!

1. Holly's Market ordered 54,123 lb of food 32 times this year. How many pounds of food did the market order in all this year?

2. Julio bought 5 bags of vegetables that each weighed $3\frac{1}{2}$ pounds. How many pounds did his purchase weigh in all?

3. Bruce paid a total of $50.80 for 8 model rocket kits. He bought them for himself and his other friends in his scout troop. How much did he pay for each rocket kit?

4. Four schools brought a total of 2,276 champion math students to the national conference on how kids can make math more fun! How many students attended from each school?

5. At the pound, $\frac{3}{7}$ of the dogs were poodles. Of the poodles, $\frac{2}{5}$ were white and fluffy. What fraction of the dogs were fluffy white poodles?

Choosing the Operation

6. Monica arrives for school at 8:15 a.m. She spends all day at school except for the 1 hour and 15 minutes that she leaves campus to attend her drama class. She leaves school at 4:30 p.m. How many hours does Monica spend at school in all?

7. An average of 6.8 of the rainy days in Purple Frog had 3.91 inches of rain. How much rain is this in all?

8. Jennifer picked $\frac{2}{7}$ of an ounce of flowers from her garden on Tuesday. On Wednesday, she picked another $\frac{3}{21}$ of an ounce. How many ounces in all did she pick?

9. Eight bags of fresh roasted peanuts were purchased for the kids watching the over-sized trucks trying to climb the mud hills! Each child was given $\frac{1}{3}$ of a bag of peanuts. How many children did these bags of peanuts serve?

10. Russell bought $9\frac{2}{5}$ lb of food for his tegu lizard, his toco toucan and his pretty, little kitty cat. He also bought $3\frac{4}{5}$ lb of vegetables and fruit for himself. How many pounds of food did he buy in all?

11. The circulation of the *Podunk Times* is 382,194 copies per edition. The closest newspaper is the *Green Leaf Gazette*, which has a circulation of 96,215 newspapers per edition. How many more newspapers does the *Podunk Times* print for each edition?

HELP-AT-HOME ACTIVITIES

Below are some activities to do with your child at home.

1. Take a picture of your child. Write height and weight on back. Repeat once a month. Write problems to compare the heights and weights.
2. Compare prices of items at the grocery store. Decide which is the best buy, etc.
3. Do 4 math word problems using something in your kitchen. Example: 50 beans divided by 5 beans equals?
4. Read a newspaper article that deals with numbers and graphs. Make up problems with the numbers and graphs.
5. Play popcorn math. Example: You have $3\frac{1}{2}$ cups, you ate $\frac{1}{4}$ cup. How many cups are left over?
6. Measure a room together.
7. Write a math word problem whose answer is equal to today's date.
8. Figure out how many hours, minutes and seconds he/she will be awake today.
9. Give your child a ruler to measure his/her leg, foot, hand, arm, etc.
10. Figure out how many days, hours and minutes there are until his/her birthday.
11. Use candy to make math problems.
12. Use holiday themes to make up word problems. Example: 32 gingerbread men ate 12 candy canes each. How many candy canes was this altogether?
13. Look at a recipe. Have him/her double and triple the recipe. Make sure it contains fractions.
14. Look at a grocery ad. Tell your child he/she can spend $50. Have him/her make up a list of things to buy. Remind your child to think about the 4 food groups.
15. Figure out how many hours, minutes and seconds he/she will be in school this week. Also figure out how many hours, minutes and seconds he/she will spend on homework.
16. With coins and bills, figure out 5 different ways to make $10, $25, $50 and $100.

© 2006 Frank Schaffer Publications